Gardens, Dining Rooms and Kitchens

An evangelism and discipleship framework for ordinary churches

by Tim Smith

A simple flexible framework that doesn't tell you what to do, but should help you formulate a strategy and work through what you are already doing well, what's not so good and what you may be missing, for mission and discipleship in your context.

This edition first published in 2012 by HD Books, The Vicarage, Plymouth
PL4 9BU Great Britain

Printed in the UK by Latimer Trend & Company Limited, Plymouth
PL6 7PY Great Britain

Copyright Tim Smith 2012

ISBN: 978-0-9572062-0-5

THANK YOU

As I wrote this book several folk were very generous with their time. They put time aside to read manuscripts that were written quickly and with passion for the subject, but maybe not too carefully. A multitude of errors were changed, some parts moved chapters, bits were removed and typing errors were resolved, but most of all they encouraged me to get this finished. I can't let them take the blame for what this is, that is all mine, but without them it might have been a more forgettable read! And so I say thank you to: Stephen and Caroline Beach, Graham Hamilton, Anna Norman-Walker, David Moss, Jonathan Rowe and most especially my wife, Gill. She encouraged me to get this finished and printed, and her skill at spotting a spelling mistake is exceptional, so any errors remaining will only be because I didn't listen to her.

Special thanks also to Phil Burgess and the Architects Design Group, Plymouth, for their generous provision of a simple short video to help me initially explain "Gardens, Dining Rooms and Kitchens" to my Church from which, with their permission, some stills are used in parts of this book. The design of the house layout was all mine to make the video work, so please don't think that's all they have to offer! Also thanks to them for their Kingdom perspective in allowing the video to be used by anyone as a background to help explain the principles of the framework. If you were to watch it before reading the book it may help, and it is only 57seconds long! It can be seen and downloaded freely from *http://www.judes.org.uk/explosive-mission/*

Contents

Introduction

Why this book? With so many church leadership volumes available, why have another? The thing is, so much of the currently published material comes from very large churches, many from another continent. Lots of folk really appreciate them and are often inspired, but smaller churches can be wary of them and they just don't feel it would fit their situation. Also, the church models offered within the volumes available typically fit a particular ecclesiology that might not sit easily on your own. Finally, too often they can make church leadership such a complicated discipline that it feels only a seasoned professional can lead using the principles being outlined.

With limited resources there is still an urgent need for the Church to become all that God wants of it, and if complication hinders that, maybe we need something that is simple, which can both be understood and put into practice by a whole church, not just the leaders? In lean times with short resources, now might be a good time to increase the workers in the harvest. If you wanted to encourage others to think through the material here, there is an accompanying Small Group Study available. This might enable a selected church team, or the whole community, to utilise the material and engage in reviewing your journey so far. Then, together see how you might want to tie in with God's mission a bit more strategically than many of us currently do.

I hope this book avoids the difficulties of poor fit or complication and yet still inspires us to try something instead of feeling we cannot achieve. There is the truth that it will be Jesus who builds his church, but he does need us to take the part he asks us to fulfil.

Therefore I have tried to distil some simple overarching ideas that I know are easily understood by a congregation because we have been getting used to them at the church I lead, a normal family oriented fellowship, St Jude's in Plymouth, UK. And I have said publically in our fellowship that I don't believe we will grow into some huge church through this work. Instead we will continue to do what this church has done for decades: grow disciples. The thing with doing this is that a proportion do leave to go and do what God wants for them elsewhere. It is sometimes frustrating when your best people move on, but it's a great Kingdom focus and you bless them on their way. Imagine what the worldwide church would be like if Antioch in Acts 13 had said to Saul and Barnabus, 'actually guys, we think it would be better if you stayed here'!

A phrase I use about this fellowship is that it punches above its weight. For the numbers here it shouldn't be able to do all it does or influence our city in the way it has, but that is what a large core of people devoted to Jesus can achieve. We aren't perfect and not everyone is Christ-like, far from it. However, having a discipling strategy is continuing what has already been done here, but now in a way that is a little more focused and built to suit today's culture and needs. This is not about growing a church's numbers necessarily, instead it is about a church trying to partner better with God for his Kingdom and his glory.

So as you proceed through this book, I have tried to keep the theology simple to support the framework described later. I felt we needed some clear theology to explain why the ideas are required to deal with a conundrum, which I outline later, sits at the heart of what I feel needs addressing. Without this background it could feel like a management journal on how to influence and grow people. But I hope we avoid that as we go through this volume together and can see that it is all about joining in with God's own heart. Therefore, I have tried to keep anything academic to a minimum as many others explain the theology of mission far more eruditely than I could, and most of us don't really need that level of detail.

This is deliberately not a set of projects or ministries that need to be followed either. This is why I don't consider the content of this book just speaks to my own church tradition, though I'm not sure you can say I have one. If I were to label myself I'm probably an open evangelical charismatic with a Roman Catholic root!

At its core this short volume deals with a conundrum I realised existed for every church. It was in tackling that big question, and being exposed to ideas and insights from a whole variety of other generous churches who shared what they had discovered, that I came to realise there was an answer that could be simply understood by a whole church, and, more importantly, could be acted upon.

An additional aim is to help you see what you already do well in your own church setting, and to use it in a more effective way for the purposes of God's Kingdom. Also, to help envisage what you can plan to do in the future when resources are available. I suspect the same principle that unfolds throughout this volume will also help you to see ministries and activities you currently run that don't contribute much, or maybe anything, to your local Kingdom growth. There may well be things you are doing that you could stop, and that can't be a bad thing with so many of our churches struggling with 'busyness'.

Whenever we are involved in smaller churches, we need to be smart with resources and everyone needs to be onboard. I hope you will find this will help you do what you do efficiently with what you have and avoid wasting effort.

Often our resources are restricted, and working smarter instead of harder, with the help of many hands, has got to be a good idea for the future of Christ's church, wherever you are.

In so many ways this is just an amalgamation of lots of different ideas from other peoples' great work. I am reminded of "Connections", a BBC TV series hosted by James Burke in the late 1970's which looked at incidents in the history of science and invention that had to have happened prior to some modern day innovations: without the prior work, the new couldn't have happened. So much of this volume has needed others to have bright ideas and insights. All I feel I have done is make some connections between disparate materials. Therefore, I offer my very grateful thanks to other church leaders who have had inspiration and felt it was right to share it with others.

I hope you find this helpful and that you can use something from it to work more effectively for the glory of our Saviour.

Chapter 1

God draws in...

"In the beginning God..."

This may be the most important theological principle expounded by scripture, summed up in the first four words of the Bible.

Everything starts with him.

Whenever we start to think that we do mission we are on shaky ground. Joining in with what God is doing is a far easier place for us to be. Mission starts with the Father. It is then the Holy Spirit who draws us into the potential of this new relationship with him through everything achieved by his son, Jesus.

My own testimony would reflect this process.

I had grown up in a Roman Catholic household and had primary and secondary schooling within those faith schools. Like so many at the time, I had a childhood of spiritual obedience followed by an early adolescence of disobedience based on a disregard for God. By the time I was 13 or 14 he didn't mean anything to me and I didn't think he had any relevance for me.

I continued into my twenties with a career as a Marine Engineer Officer on seagoing oil tankers followed by a short spell at university in Manchester when I met my wife, Gill.

My career evolved into various areas of selling and engineering and I can remember an uncomfortable feeling, in my late 20's when my wife and I had a house, two cars, good jobs and overseas holidays. We were doing really well and our relationship was strong. But the feeling had to do with a sense of purpose in life itself. It was more like, 'is this what life is really for?' But it's easy to put that feeling to the back of your mind, and I did.

Then my mother had a straightforward operation that didn't turn out well, she became terminally ill and was kept in an induced coma.

Sitting at a bedside for most of a fortnight with my father and brothers was not easy. I don't mean we didn't get on or that the emotions ran high, though of course they did at times, but it is also physically draining. We all took turns to go for walks around the hospital. It was on one of those strolls that I came across the hospital's chapel.

It wasn't a foreign space for me, just one of a type I hadn't entered for a personal reason for a decade and a half. I remember feeling I should say a prayer for my mother, and there was a book I could write in, so maybe someone else would too. I suspect it was a fairly selfish prayer, but it was the first time in quite a while that I had acknowledged that God might have relevance for my life.

Then my mother died.

I know I found that hard and the funeral even more difficult. But it didn't take too long for life to become 'normal' again and I don't remember having any obvious struggles.

A few weeks later, I had a sense of a real hunger to go back to church. The odd thing was that it wasn't at all a melancholic response, it was a strange hunger. We had some friends, who invited us to dinner and I still remember the conversation about going to their church. I don't recall them inviting me, I think I asked them what time they met and could we join them soon. Interestingly, and probably very frustratingly for her, my wife had been wanting to go to church most of the time we had been together, but I seemed to have needed a greater influence to get me moving.

After a few weeks of going along to our local church, the minister invited us on a simple course for newcomers to explore faith, a bit like an early Alpha Course. So many of my childhood memories of Bible stories and childhood church teaching came flooding back and within a few short weeks it all made total sense.

It took about a year before I realised that it was God who had given me that hunger to return. His grace provided me with the 'greater influence' I had needed. I had acknowledged him for the first time in years in that hospital chapel and he, like the Father in the parable of the Prodigal Son, ran to me and drew me back to his family, the church.

My friends had been strong enough in their faith that I could know them both as friends and as people who went to church and had a faith. God would also have known the church they attended would feed me and help me to grow.

Mission starts with God and he influences us through his Holy Spirit. Of course he doesn't force or cajole us into his Kingdom, he simply places people or circumstances in front of us who might encourage us to begin to think about him. When we open the door to him a little, as I did many years ago in that hospital chapel, he is able to draw us closer to his family.

When we allow the Holy Spirit some room, scripture tells us he will lead us:

But when he, the Spirit of truth, comes, he will guide you into all truth.
(John 16:13)

The invitation God offers through the Holy Spirit is intriguing and compelling without being coercive. We see that same character of the Holy Spirit acting in Paul's life in Acts (20:23):

And now, compelled by the Spirit, I am going to Jerusalem, not knowing what will happen to me there.

As I look back at my journey's experiences, I can really relate to this verse. I was 'compelled' to return to church without any knowledge of why or of what may be the outcome. I didn't have to go, I just wanted to.

So often we don't really know why we do some things for God. We just feel God is speaking to us in some way or that it's a response to a Bible based imperative we know is meant for us to act on. It can be exactly the same for a non-churchgoer. They may not use a Christian's language, but they can still feel that they need to do something in response to a prompt from God, even if they don't know it is him.

If we recognise this characteristic of God in his actions among us it doesn't mean we leave mission to him and do nothing. Instead, it is about acknowledging that our God is a God of revelation. By accepting his actions as the grace of God, we are in a better place and won't get too puffed up thinking any results will be because of our own skill or hard work. But Jesus did leave us to do the work of mission, accompanied to the end of time by the Holy Spirit. From Matt 28:19-20, which many know as the Great Commission:

Therefore go and make disciples of all nations, baptising them in the name of the Father and of the Son and of the Holy Spirit, and teaching them to obey everything I have commanded you. And surely I am with you always, to the very end of the age.

We know, and do well to remember, that our faith is based on a God who reveals himself. We don't find him; instead he finds us, just as the shepherd looking for the lost sheep of a flock.

John affirms the importance of the draw of God in his Gospel (6:44):

No-one can come to me unless the Father who sent me draws him.

And he re-iterates it later in Jesus' words (12:32):

But I, when I am lifted up from the earth, will draw all men to myself.

This is grace in action. We can do nothing; only God can reveal himself and only God can draw us into his family. He doesn't have to and we don't deserve it, but he does. That's grace.

Because God loves us so much, he longs for us all to be part of his family, he cannot use force or coercion as it is all based on the love that he is. If God influenced us to the extent that we couldn't do anything other than do what he asks then we would see free will being diminished or lost. It seems that free will becomes the handcuffs God willingly places on himself to allow love to reign supreme.

And so he invites, he knocks on doors, he places people on our path and he raises up churches who are welcoming. This is our God of mission.

The theological impact of this concept has to be part of how we see his church operating. We cannot 'do' church our way, but only his way, because if we 'do' it our way, it will fail. The reason our way won't work is that we don't draw in, only God reveals himself and draws in.

Chapter 2

...and people connect

God draws in....

        ... and people connect.

The days of large mission events being effective are largely over in the USA and Western Europe. Friendship evangelism sits more comfortably on our shoulders and brings with it the benefit of personal testimony. Trying to convince someone on the street with a flip chart and a loud voice offering a step by step explanation of the gospel is more likely to get them to walk on the other side of the road than stand around and listen today.

However, when we tell a friend how our life changed on discovering all that Jesus means to us we get listened to more, because they know us, they know our character. Personal friendship evangelism doesn't need a coherent argument from scripture laid out as a conclusive proof; instead it begins with a relationship between two people, one sharing why their life is as it is. Expecting a stranger to expound Bible passages at them is not going to work today if the person being targeted has no relationship with the speaker, God or the Bible. Why would they trust the stranger, God or the Bible? But if they have a relationship with you, at some point they will trust you enough to hear your story, at the appropriate time, and maybe meet your other friends.

When we come alongside someone we are showing them something of our own belief, even if we don't directly share the Gospel with them. Over time, those we start friendships with, can hopefully have an opportunity to witness, through a growing acquaintance, our lives of purpose and hope that are being fulfilled within a community. The reality of those positive aspects in the life of a Christ follower can be difficult to deny when they are seen firsthand.

And we mustn't deny the power of our church communities to impact our friends or relatives. I remember when some of my family visited who weren't churchgoers. They chose to come along on a Sunday morning because I was leading the service. As normally happened at the end of the morning, folk stayed and mingled, having a cup of coffee. There were conversations between young and old, between well dressed and not so well dressed, between different nationalities. Back at home, while getting ready for Sunday lunch, they said they had felt there was a real sense of community in the church. I decided to not just agree and instead challenged them ever so slightly, to try and find out more, with something like, 'Well, it's not that special, you can get it in any club where folk get together, like a golf club or something.'

However they didn't agree, but said instead it was 'something special'. They found the people in my church rather attractive and beyond what they expected. By the way, I do too, but they are just normal folk of a normal mixture who do normal things. And just in case they read this and start to get big headed, it is not them, that's the Holy Spirit in action!

When we build friendships we build trust as well. But it takes time, sometimes one at a time, and one at a time isn't a bad thing.

Howard Schultz is the founder of Starbucks and he had loosed the reigns over the years for others to lead the company. But he began to feel the organisation was losing its way in the mid 1990's and decided he had to come back and take over the leadership of the global enterprise as CEO. In his book which recounts that story and the reclaiming of the founding principles and subsequent growth of the company, Howard recognised that the growth wasn't sustainable and that they needed to get back to ensuring each cup of coffee brewed met the needs of each customer.[1]

He realised that the organisation had lost its perspective on what they were about: they were chasing profit first. Instead his dream had always been about making good quality coffee that people wanted to gather with their friends to drink, which was also profitable. They sold coffee and connections, not just a product at a price. For the company to succeed, each connection had to work with each coffee.

Our Churches are in a similar 'business' in some ways. We connect to each other and to God in loving relationships that are individual, and both horizontal and vertical. The Great Commandments outline that principle in our need to love one another and to love God. To try and do that without thinking about how we relate individually to each other means we may lose our own direction as churches. And for it to work, a church needs

---

[1] 2011 Howard Schultz *Onward* John Wiley & Sons Pg 152

to understand how important these singular relationships are. It was Mother Theresa who apparently said, 'God hasn't called us to do great things, but to do small things with great love'. Helping people one at a time in Calcutta was crucial when surrounded by so many needing help. When it comes to reaching lost people, there are millions, but we meet them one at a time, and we need to do so with honesty, with love.

We can concentrate on building a church, or we can concentrate on helping people who don't know Jesus become his followers. If we follow building the church and forget the founder's principles based on people being alongside people it won't last. But if we recognise his desire to reach the world, one lost sheep at a time, and structure ourselves around the core intention of God's values why should it fail?

One at a time the world can be changed.

It might not sound as exciting as getting dozens of people coming to faith at some event, and that might still happen occasionally, but most things in our churches change slowly, step by step, one at a time.

This ethos contrasts with the large evangelistic events of the mid 20th century. Over the twelve weeks of Billy Graham's Harringay Crusade in London in 1954 some 1,750,000 people attended[2]. But then there was the pull of a famous and charismatic American evangelist in an era of austerity. The majority of the population

---

[2]http://www.billygraham.org.uk/Groups/174527/Billy_Graham_Evangelistic/Who_We_Are/About_Us/1954_Harringay/1954_ Harringay.aspx

didn't have access to distractions like the TV in the way we have today. The population of the UK was still open to Christianity in the post war years and there would have been few families with more than one generation of non-churchgoing. Today, there is little chance of similar outreach being successful here. Relational mission is the key in Western cultures today.

But relationships don't just start, they evolve. Sometimes we refer to one of our closest friends as if they were family and that sort of friendship doesn't just happen. Think back over some of your own closest friends. How did you meet, what type of things brought you closer together?

So often we meet through coincidence with someone else being the catalyst. I wouldn't have met my wife Gill, if my closest school friend hadn't stayed in a particular hall of residence while he was at Manchester University. I was working at sea as an engineer on oil tankers and would come home on leave for two or three months at a time. He and I had kept in touch by post and it was obvious we would catch up when I was on leave. He had a different circle of friends from those we had known in our school days, but they welcomed me along on nights out. I was welcomed in as a guest. Over time many of them became great friends, but Gill became family.

One at a time connections can be transformational as guests can turn into friends and a smaller number become family.

My times with Jesus has been the same.

If my parents hadn't been churchgoers I wouldn't have known him as early as I did. To begin with, my primary school days were about classes and playing with mates. I can still remember my first day at school. I wouldn't have used the word then, but the feelings are the same as when you're a guest among a group of people you don't yet know. But the friendships began and as the school was linked to a church there were also regular times in services during the week and again on Sundays with the family. By about the age of eight I can remember knowing God was real. I helped as an altar boy in that little Catholic Church, maybe ringing a bell at the right moment in the communion prayers or even better, and far more fun at the time, swinging some incense.

And so began my friendship with Jesus, though it was a little flawed I now realise. At the time I had a fear of God, but it wasn't fear of God in the biblical sense, but in an eight year old's sense. One moment in particular is vivid still for me because of my lack of understanding of what that church believed. The priest asked me to take the chalice from the vestry to the altar in the church before the service began. It was covered by a cloth and he reminded me not to touch the chalice, but to just hold it through the cloth. I'm sure he didn't expect his words to spark my imagination they way they did. Well, I had seen those Bible pictures of Uzzah (1 Chronicles 13:9) touching the ark and being zapped! I had never carried anything so carefully. That's what I mean by an eight year old's fear of God.

So, I had an introduction to Jesus' family as a guest and an initial friendship of sorts, even though flawed. In my case it was followed by a gap when I allowed my friendship with Jesus to just lapse. But again as is the case for some, when we rediscover a good friendship, it moves into a much closer thing and we see it evolve into a family tie. It was the same for me as I came to see Jesus for who he is, accepted him and became part of the family of God. We move from being a guest of a community into becoming a friend of some members of that group and we find ourselves getting adopted into the family of God.

Human relationships with each other evolve from guests to friends and sometimes from friendship to family, and the same things happen with God.

The point of the later chapters that unfold, *Gardens, Dining Rooms and Kitchens*, is that they reflect the same evolving relationship pattern that is available with the Father as we get introduced to his Son as a guest. An invitation enabled and made enticing by the Holy Spirit.

As we get to meet with Jesus and his family and friends, we realise we too can be a part of this crowd of friends and they are, I hope, such a different crowd from what we expected, friendly and interested in us. For some of us, we realise that their friendship is more than that. They love us because they know what real love is: they have discovered grace.

Through them and their care, helped by the Holy Spirit, as we open a door for Jesus, we discover a long lost brother and we can move from the guest who became a friend into a family member.

It's a bit like the TV reality shows where twins separated at birth get re-united: the hug we get from Jesus is just as real as we get connected again and are once more a part of the family.

This partnership with the Holy Spirit doesn't just mean we invite, and the Holy Spirit makes it interesting. Probably more often it is that we are prompted at the right moment to say something to a friend which they then find enticing. For that to happen more frequently we undoubtedly need to be more aware of the voice of the Holy Spirit, to be able to trust him and his timing.

All this I have spoken while still with you. But the Counsellor, the Holy Spirit, whom the Father will send in my name, will teach you all things and will remind you of everything I have said to you. (John 14:25-26)

If we are to partner with the Holy Spirit we need to learn to recognise his voice, as the sheep of the shepherd are supposed to (John 10:27), and listen for his voice. As we read in each of the seven churches of Revelation:

He who has an ear, let him hear what the Spirit says to the churches'

This is a regularly repeated phrase of Jesus, 'he who has an ear, let him hear'[3]. Each of the Gospel evangelists quote Jesus using these words. For us to connect with people at the right time, we need to hear the prompting of God, and act on it.

If God draws in, then we can connect sometimes. But the perfect occasion and the perfect opportunity will always be when the Holy Spirit prompts us. Then hopefully, your friend will also find the invitation to take a step somewhere with you enticing.

---

[3] Matthew 11:15, 13:9, 13:43, Mark 4:9, 7:16, Luke 8:8, 14:35, Revelation of John 2:7, 2:11, 2:17, 2:29, 3:6, 3:13, 3:22 & 13:9

Chapter 3

Mission isn't enough...

If the thought of evangelism fills you with dread, I think you are going to read what I have to say next and possibly despair...

...mission isn't enough, there is more we need to do.

Sorry about that.

But I promise, hang in there because it does all get simpler.

Churches can be active in their evangelistic efforts and in their desire to grow disciples, but all too often mission and spiritual growth are disassociated disciplines or may not both present in the same church.

So let us see as we move on, if we can agree with having the last major instruction from Jesus at the heart of our aim as a church globally. Matthew 28:19-20 outlines the Great Commission:

Therefore go and make disciples of all nations, baptising them in the name of the Father and of the Son and of the Holy Spirit, and teaching them to obey everything I have commanded you.

Often evangelical churches take the word 'go' as a crucial and central message, and it is very important, but is it the most or only important thing in Jesus' last command?

Teaching newcomers to the faith "everything" Jesus commanded his first disciples is a firmly linked command along with His missional one of "go".

While we read, *"go and make disciples of all nations, baptising them in the name of the Father and of the Son and of the Holy Spirit, and teaching them to obey everything I have commanded you"*, we don't know where we need to make any extra emphasis, if any. If I were to ask you to "Go to the shop and buy food", what would be the most important of the instructions, 'go' or 'buy'? In this rather awkwardly written sentence you could suggest 'buying food' is just as important as 'going', though common sense would suggest there isn't much point in going if you don't buy the food!

Using common sense, along with the imperative Greek verbs, we can recognise there is a need for more than just going. Both could be of similar importance, but it is quite easy to suggest there is a greater imperative in the Great Commission, to *'make disciples of all nations, baptising them and teaching them to obey everything I (Jesus) have commanded you.'*

Therefore, we have to look seriously at making disciples as well as mission. But one thing has bothered me in this whole area of helping people grow to become more like Jesus. Why do we so often take a long view about making disciples, how biblical is that? Should it be that complicated?

I have often wondered about the rapid growth of the early church without Theology Colleges and 'professional' ministers. How could the church have grown so rapidly? It almost seems that Paul just strode into town, taught for a while, maybe up to a year, then set up some local leaders in a small community and went onto the next town. He might have visited again or written them a letter, but in essence it was that simple, and over the next century the growth of the church was exponential. And that growth was in the main down to the people Paul encountered, not Paul directly. To our modern minds it doesn't sound like much of a plan!

My own experience of becoming a minister within the Church of England suggests we would never achieve it if God decided to grow his Kingdom exponentially again. To explain, I had my first thoughts that God might be calling me into a full time church leadership, but it took me some six months to decide that this was a strong enough sense that God might be calling me to actually apply. I wasn't that quick on the uptake.

There then followed a whole year when I was asked to meet with others who had similar thoughts. The selection process took another 2 or 3 years to be told that the Church recognised my sense of call but they weren't sure I was right for the role.

Some would say unfortunately for the Church, God didn't stop prompting me as I applied again about two years later and was offered college training and then four years as a curate (a training post with an experienced church leader).

After I felt that first call from God it was twelve years before I took up my first post as a church leader. And I wasn't starting as a fresh faced convert in the beginning either, but someone who had been leading small groups, giving some talks at evening gatherings, part of a church leadership council and everything else we all do.

Can you imagine what the outcome for the Kingdom would have been if that had been the model in Paul's day?

Would it surprise you that Paul did have an opinion on how long it should take to form a disciple well enough to be a significant part within God's Kingdom, someone who could feed themselves and others?

In 1 Corinthians we read a letter from Paul to a community that scholars believe could not have been written more than three or four years after he had been with them for some months. In Chapter 3, verses 1 & 2 we read him saying:

I could not address you as spiritual but as worldly—mere infants in Christ. I gave you milk, not solid food, for you were not yet ready for it. Indeed, you are still not ready.

Paul had wanted the people he met to have been further along than when he was with them and now, only three or four years later at most, we can feel his disappointment still. Paul seemed to want people to be able to move from being fed to being able to feed themselves and others within maybe four years, and that for some was from a standing start as a pagan.

And Paul wasn't alone in this aspiration.

God's plan for this world's redemption was to send Jesus. God knew as the Holy Spirit commissioned Jesus in the Jordan that three years later Jesus would be able to give the victory cry of an accomplished task - "It is finished!"

That meant there would only be three years for the disciples to go from being tax collectors and fishermen to becoming the leaders of a new religious movement. At the beginning of their walk with Jesus they weren't biblical scholars or significant people in their synagogues: these were just ordinary local folk like most people who come to our churches. In fact the primary question Jesus had of Peter before he asked him to lead the church was not about education or theological knowledge, but instead, "Do you love me?" (John 21:15-17). Jesus seems far more interested in our relationship with him and our character than our educational standing. Sadly, I don't remember ever being asked that question during my interviews for full time ministry either.

I believe that we are called to go out to connect with the people God is drawing to himself, and then, and most importantly, to teach them all we can, quickly.

I am convinced we shall see fruit if we help people in their relationships with Jesus and each other. As we explore later, in enabling others to follow the Great Commandments, to love God and each other more, that we shall also see disciples evolve who can grow the kingdom in unison with God in his mission.

Regarding Paul's regret about the spiritual growth of the Corinthians, it can be seen as a metaphor. Milk is a foodstuff that is always pre-digested by someone else, a cow or a mother. We could see milk as second hand learning, when someone else is needed to digest scripture then give it out in a simpler digestible form. But Paul seems to suggest that he expected there to be a way we can be first hand learners, or meat eaters, much sooner than we often experience today.

The difficulty with the milk and solid food analogy is that Paul is trying to show these adults they shouldn't be on 'milk' anymore: in other words, that they should be feeding themselves spiritually with 'solid food'. But the church often seems to look on spiritual growth as if we grow as disciples in the same way we grow from an infant through a childhood and adolescence into an adult from milk to solid food.

I used the following analogy a few years back of the growth of a child from a baby to an adult to illustrate our current difficulty if we don't take Paul's analogy correctly.

At birth and for at least 6 months a baby can only rely on milk, food that is pre-digested by its mother before being re-delivered as milk. At this early stage the baby cannot, and is not expected to be able to feed itself. But at about 6 months we start to offer it the very first simple solid foods.

Patently for a human child to go out to work to earn the money that buys the food isn't practical. Once they start to eat solid food, they still need someone to provide it. I don't think this is the solid food Paul meant. He was writing to adults and using milk as a soft diet option, necessary in the beginning but not long term. And patently he couldn't have expected the real human child to adult transition within three years, he means spiritually.

But, in many ways the church's inherited model in lots of places is to maintain the provision of solid food in the same way as we feed a young person, instead of seeing our church members as people who should be helped to feed themselves and then others.

I found this picture summed up so many of our churches today: a lot of people who can eat solid food. These are significant meat eaters, yet they are people who are unable to supply themselves with their own sustenance. These children needed their parents to wake them and tell them when to go to school and when to stay home. They needed the food for their breakfast bought by their parents and put on the table, the school meals were sourced and cooked by others and Mum presented a wonderful meal at the end of the day without thanks. While they could eat meat, I don't believe these are the meat eaters Paul hoped for. (By the way, that's my own old school photo. I'm second from left on the front row!)

If you think about your own church, does this sound familiar? Do you still spoon feed people who should be able to feed themselves?

Paul can't have meant 'solid food' eaters were like these children. He had only two categories of people, milk drinkers and meat eaters, so what was Paul expecting?

Maybe he hoped that within a few years, three or four at the most, the people he left behind in Corinth would have been able to be meat eaters, people who could not just consume solid teaching, but also not to have to rely on others like Paul to provide it for them.

It hadn't happened though for the Corinthians, which is why Paul is disappointed. But it does seem to have been what he thought should and could have been the outcome.

In many of our churches we don't even aim for it and therefore we will always miss this mark. I do recognise that even if we aim for it, we might still miss it and the time span may well be longer than three years for some, but at least it won't be twenty! Some will progress and some won't, but we should plan to help those who are willing to grow to do so. We need to enable those who want to follow Christ to do so.

Therefore we need to structure our churches with some sort of framework that helps lead people to a place where they can be self sustaining within a few years. I believe that, with no structure we are planning for such poor growth that we might simply fail.

Some may raise the point that Paul did write to Timothy (1 Tim 3:6) about Overseers and Deacons not being recent converts:

He must not be a recent convert, or he may become conceited and fall under the same judgment as the devil.

But what did Paul mean by a 'recent convert'? He can't have meant how we interpret it so much today or with 1st century life spans they would all have died before the gospel spread! And, Paul is talking of a leading role, of what today we might call Bishops or Church leaders. It doesn't mean that before that point they wouldn't be expected to be active in their faith, fulfilled in their worship, in complete fellowship with others, seeing themselves growing as disciples with ministries in their community and involved in evangelism in their neighbourhood.

Recent very large scale research[4]. shows the need for not delaying encouraging a new churchgoer with some discipleship programs. One finding was very interesting: If people attend your church without making a significant commitment to Jesus before about five years[5], then they are unlikely to do so at all.

And you may wonder, what did their research offer as a solution? Well, they were also able to identify churches that were doing well at enabling growing disciples and these churches had some things in common, one being a leader who is determined and focused in

---

[4] REVEAL, one of 3 volumes, *REVEAL* (2007), *Follow Me* (2008) and *Focus* (2009) published by The Willow Creek Association all by Greg Hawkins and Cally Parkinson

[5] 2001 Greg Hawkins and Cally Parkinson *Move* Zondervan Page 19

helping folk become disciples of Jesus. I hope this book may help you in that area. The fact that you are reading around the topic of church leadership means that you want to improve and learn more. Keep it up.

We can become insular in our reading and learning and maintaining a wide remit can enable strands to be drawn together that were not anticipated in one context, but that can make a major shift in understanding when linked with another. I can only say from personal experience that this has happened in my own reading over the years. Links get formed that can be very helpful.

Other suggested factors that link spiritually healthy churches may be more significant for us in this context. In terms of spiritual disciplines, the most important thing we can help our people with, is to encourage them to regularly reflect on scripture for themselves. Interestingly if we were to all do this one thing, reflecting on God's word for our own benefit, we become, using Paul's analogy, meat eaters.

Reflecting on scripture on our own could fulfil the simple definition of a meat eater because as we read scripture alone and dwell on it, the things that excite or convict us are the solid food we need, and this will be provided directly to us by the action of the Holy Spirit through our reading and contemplation. Maybe this is why this one spiritual discipline is so important. Paul recognised that self-feeding is a major measure of a disciple, and being helped, encouraged and enabled to regularly reflect on scripture should enable us to feed ourselves.

Another finding was the churches that were seeing a larger percentage of stronger disciples had structure for new members.

They had courses that new members know are available to them as they joined their communities. This same point is backed up in recent research among Church of England clergy[6].

Therefore, we can see that the action of the Holy Spirit is crucial in mission as it is God in his grace who draws folk toward himself. But he also requires us to do our part in mission by connecting in real relational ways with those we encounter. And with the realisation that mission isn't enough, we begin to recognise we also need discipleship training in place.

But this realisation led me into the conundrum I have come to see is at the heart of the church's problem and it is one that we all need to discover our own way of answering in our own local contexts…

---

[6] Pg 9 Church of England & Kings College London "Experiences of Ministry Survey" Nov 2011

Chapter 4

The Conundrum

*While we may 'do' outreach, it is the Holy Spirit who
encourages someone towards a church so they can both encounter
Jesus **and** grow in Him. If the church can't offer that
discipleship, why would the Holy Spirit bring them?*

I have always quite liked the word 'conundrum', unlike the word
'problem'.

I suspect, when we approach a 'problem' we mostly start with a
negative image of the task ahead of us. But if we are engaged in
solving a 'conundrum' we're a bit more relaxed. It feels like it is a
safe and comfortable word, maybe even fun..

When we looked at why people attend events there are often a
few things at work. For instance a plainly typed invitation to an
event may give all the relevant information, but will it excite
anyone's imagination? In marketing there is an acrostic for the
stages someone goes through before they take action on a
decision, it's A.I.D.A., like the opera. It stands for:

A   arousal
I   interest
D   desire
A   action

For someone to begin to respond to an invitation we need to catch their attention, or *A*rouse them. Then there needs to be enough to get them *I*nterested to bring about a *D*esire that may be significant for them to take *A*ction and come to your event.

This is the case for an invite to a secular event or to try and persuade someone to buy something.

As an example I used to host parties with my friend in the student flat we occupied in the early 1980's. We put a lot of effort into our invites and it meant they stood out. Our parties were always packed.

I remember one invite was an imitation of a British bank note, with serious modification I must admit: even we knew you can't go around copying them. One phrase on a real note is: 'We promise to pay the bearer the sum of Five Pounds' … or ten or twenty depending on the note. Our invite currency instead had the phrase, 'We promise to give the bearer a good time'. Another theme was similar to the opening pages of JRR Tolkien's book, 'The Lord Of The Rings'. It was of his first chapter called 'A Long Expected Party'. It was complete with our version of Tolkien's hand drawn map of Hobbiton in the Shire, except in our case, it was directions to our flat. Alongside our map were the opening paragraphs of the story of our party that we hoped was still to unfold on the night. A third I know is still remembered by some old friends. It was a fully working copy of a well known flip top cigarette packet that took us weeks to resolve with two passes through an early photocopier with black ink followed by a second pass with red ink. There were no colour copiers in those days. They were assembled and given out and that party was packed, and folk kept the invite.

I see such an obvious parallel to a well thought up and intriguing party invitation to the action with the Holy Spirit when we work in partnership with him, and invite someone to be a guest at something the church may have put on.

The Holy Spirit brings the intrigue factor to un-churched people and provides all the *AID* we need, the *A*rousal, *I*nterest, and he gives some influence over the *D*esire, though he will never force the *A*ction. It will always be our choice whether we respond.

I have lost count of conversations with people I meet who have turned up at church services who have said something like, "I don't really know why I'm here, but I wanted to come along". At some point they have accepted an invitation or seen an advert or just turned up because they had a feeling or were simply interested to come and see. I don't think that's normal behaviour.

A quick question.

Have you ever just gone into a squash club because you had a feeling? How about a political or trade union club? And yet people do turn up at a church just because they were passing. It is odd behaviour, but they do. That has to be the Holy Spirit with a gentle tug at their hearts.

We all know that God does want us to play our part in his mission. It might be a personal invitation, a well designed outward facing and friendly website or even something as simple as a tidy car park. All these sorts of things are really important if we are to help the Holy Spirit as he touches someone's heart. We need to help him and not hinder him.

Mission requires us to go to those who don't know Jesus. Sometimes we can get the feeling that if only we could get this right that we would see our churches grow. But it is also seen as one of the hardest things for a church to do. How do you do it? We can see so many obstacles when we think about structuring church evangelism that sometimes we don't start. Evangelism brings up images of knocking on doors or standing on a street handing out tracts, or maybe learning a five point explanation of the Gospel and engineering a conversation so you can share it.

Am I close in describing what you fear most?

If I said I was going to show you just such a method you would probably close the book now with a shiver down your spine.

But to restate my conundrum: if Jesus wants followers and the Father sends the Holy Spirit to encourage someone to take a step towards himself as he begins to reveal himself to them, why would he draw them to a church where they won't be helped to become followers?

Therefore, if evangelism can be simplified to 'joining in with God's mission', then it is always important to recognise the very large part the Holy Spirit has with each individual as they begin their journey back to their Father. But, we must include within the intention of the Father, that he also longs for them to become disciples of his Son.

Mission and discipleship must be linked.

Some of our churches put huge pressure on their members to be involved in local mission programs, distributing tracts from door to door or holding street evangelism in their local shopping centre with a group trying to make it look like there is an interested crowd around an average speaker with a flip chart. Maybe instead in the past we have invited a well known speaker and the congregation had to invite their friends. Unfortunately the speaker is only well known in the churches, our friends don't know them, so we don't invite anyone, because we like to keep our friends!

Whichever outreach method was used, often we didn't see much fruit, just uncomfortable congregants, embarrassed friends and annoyed neighbours.

And there are other churches who might not do much outreach but put great emphasis and energy into discipling their folk, maybe to work for the poor and give generously. Often they might not see much growth either.

But some mission minded churches which do see growth also seem to offer great help and guidance so that those who join them know there is a path available[7] to them: one that they can choose to join; a path that can result in a closer relationship with their Father through Jesus their brother, enabled by their guide, the Holy Spirit.

So, if the Holy Spirit is part of the invitation process, why would he invite folk where they can't be helped to become more like Jesus?

---

[7] Pg 9 Church of England & Kings College London "Experiences of Ministry Survey" Nov 2011

We know from scripture that the Holy Spirit is active on behalf of Jesus, inviting people to follow him. We can begin with a look at Jesus, having just been filled with the Holy Spirit, saying to the first disciples:

"Come, follow me," Jesus said, "and I will make you fishers of men."
(Matthew 4:19)

It is an intriguing invitation, just as intriguing as those he makes today.

Imagine Simon (Peter) and Andrew fishing when this stranger invites them to go and join him and fish for men. It is difficult to think how we might have responded if we were in their shoes. But then, I suppose it was Jesus who had very recently been anointed by the Holy Spirit asking. Also, notice the content of his call to follow Him - *"and I will make you fishers of men"*

Within Jesus' call is the plain upfront statement of how he will help them to change and grow into a new 'career', as fishers of men. Jesus had a discipleship plan in place: he called, and the Holy Spirit brought the intrigue factor because Jesus' timing was perfect. Then they came.

Today I believe it is the same and research appears to back it up.

When the provision for someone to grow exists in a church, the Holy Spirit can initiate the prompt that gets it all in motion and begin to bring people, even sometimes without our obvious involvement.

Have you ever done a significant outreach of some sort and seen what you feel are poor results? Did you have something in place for those who might have responded? Did you have further discipleship planned into your church long term after that for them and your whole church?

So before we move on to thinking of strategies, can we just look at maybe the biggest problem churches face when they want to move forward in some way...

Chapter 5

The workers are few

"The harvest is plentiful but the workers are few. Ask the Lord of the harvest, therefore, to send out workers into his harvest field."
Matthew 9:37-38

You want to move forward with a new ministry or strategy, but wonder who you can ask. Do you have the feeling that in the past the Church has forgotten about this passage? That the work of the many has instead been restricted to the few?

Sometimes it has been the fault of controlling Ministers who need to keep tight reins on everything their church does, so much so that they become the restricting and limiting factor. Or there are congregations who have expected the Pastor to be the only one who visits the poor and sickly, does the news sheet and service cards, arranges fundraising, runs a youth club and be a good husband or wife for their partner, parent their children to a godly standard and preach a phenomenal sermon each week as well!

Historically, in many churches of all sorts of all denominations, lay involvement (I have to say I really don't like that phrase as it suggests difference) wasn't encouraged unless you were looking after the buildings or the money. The result was overworked clergy and overfed congregants in churches that were under-resourced. It then leaves a tired leader unable to provide vision or see how to be the body of Christ together.

Today there is a new language of 'collaboration' between ordained and lay to try and encourage a sharing of some of the ministries, although I still smile whenever I hear the word, as a collaborator used to be a definition of someone who worked with the enemy! I much prefer partnerships or teams. However, the intention behind the word is to work together. The problem can be that, because of the decades of the prior models, we don't know how to partner in these common goals in any planned or strategic way. Hopefully we can begin to change that by the end of this book.

Individuals in churches often have good ideas for lots of disparate things we might do, but will they all help in the aim of the church? How can we encourage these ideas people to be focused on what will help grow the church?

I know almost everyone wants to reach out and raise up disciples who will love God more each day and love their neighbour with increasing resolve. We long for the day when those same people become devoted disciples and begin to replicate what they learned to new folk they have met. We hope to begin the cycle again for another generation who will then do the same. But too often we don't think we have the resources, we don't know what to do next and we go into maintenance mode instead, which in reality means a slow death.

But Jesus suggested that there will be a need for a quantity of 'workers' to reach the 'harvest'. Surely he will have ensured the resources are available to us somehow, somewhere?

This need for us to find a way of effective collaborative ministry may be helped if we look first at Peter's affirmation of all believers (1 Peter 2:9):

You are a chosen people, a royal priesthood, a holy nation, a people belonging to God, that you may declare the praises of him who called you out of darkness into his wonderful light.

Priests are the intermediaries between people and God. The chosen people, ourselves, have a duty to bring about an introduction between those who don't know Jesus and their creator. This passage is not just about 'ordained' people, but instead the whole nation of believers, the priests of this holy nation. These are the workers that Jesus wants to see sent out, you and me.

Churches may need professionally trained leaders in some circumstances. I'm one, but my dream is to make myself redundant and leave a church that can simply carry on without me and become a marvellously functioning, growing, self replicating and repairing local Body of Christ.

When it comes to being a part of the body I have often been asked how I see myself. Well, to begin with, I am not the head, that's most definitely Jesus Christ, and I am not the neck, the single conduit through which Jesus leads, maybe that is the Holy Spirit. I often feel I am more like the left elbow, connected structurally enough to the frame to be able to nudge and pull the community but not able to drag it off in any direction or make it run when it's not ready.

Without a whole church operating as the Body of Christ the church won't operate at all well. If the foot absents itself we will limp along. If the legs go, we must just sit where we are. We need each other and we all need to sing off the same hymn sheet. By having a strategy that can be easily expounded so it is quickly understandable and adopted by all the Body, we can start to do more than just limp along.

We know in many of our churches the workers are few. One of the primary aims of this book is to offer a simplified way of looking at what we may need to do, that is easily understood and assimilated, so that everyone can join in and see a direction that is positive and give some hope. In time we can be the many so that we can join in with God's Mission to his world.

But before we all run off to do things together, we need to know what we are running towards.

Chapter 6

The Aim: C4 Church

And so we come to the part to which the prior chapters have been leading. I felt we needed some foundations to explain why we needed a strategy for both outreach and personal and group spiritual growth, before we actually started to look at how it might work as a strategy.

We know we need more 'workers in the vineyard', that this is not just desirable, but biblical. We can also see we have an ongoing conundrum, that in some way we need to be proactive in both mission and discipleship and we recognised that in mission we partner with God who draws in folk and who needs us to connect with them. We also know that we need to structure our churches to allow a new Christian to become a follower of Jesus within a few years, not a few decades.

I took a few chapters to expand that, but we can't expect a church congregation to remember all of that all the time. We need simple aims to begin with that help sum it all up and that can then sustain a simple strategy. What is the core of the aim of the church? Can we get it to a short and memorable sentence?

In the summer before I took up my post in Plymouth, I was fortunate enough to have a few weeks in Provence, France. I spent a large amount of that time trying to find the words that would sum up what that aim would be as I led this new community. I came up with C4 Church.

I was very taken a few years earlier by recognising that my role as a church leader was to ensure I did my best to keep the church I might lead stay attentive to God and not to me. If I was going to achieve that, I knew I would need something to keep both me and the church focused in our attention

Having a focus as a Pastor on helping people become devoted Christ followers is just a 'no brainer', isn't it? As a slight aside, I find it interesting that we use the word 'pastor' or 'pastoral' for a church leader sometimes, when we want that warm feeling that there is someone going to come alongside us for cosy chats. The problem with the shepherd analogy is we have a modern romantic view of it that I'm not convinced is historical or biblical.

Shepherds were tough characters who made sure the sheep were accounted for, which is why they knew if 1 in 100 was missing (Luke 15:4) and they were there to fight the bears and lions! (1 Sam 17:34) Therefore, a church leader needs the same determination and focus on their aim, to ensure the sheep are safe in the pen. That is a shepherd's first and most important job. In the same way, a church needs this strong focus.

So I came to realise the urgency of the need for a church to be involved in outreach and growing disciples, along with true fellowship and a growing love of God. I also knew I required the aim to be resolved with a phrase that could be easily remembered by the church. This was going to be the 'why', but not yet the 'how'.

As I struggled with many variations I could see an opportunity to create a block of words where the significant ones began with 'C'. And to make it even better, there were four of them, the first of which was Christ, which is a great place to start. But why are four 'C's a good thing I hear you ask - because C4 has the potential to explode!

Therefore, the aim was to be a community that is about:

CHRIST
AND OUR
COMMITMENT
TO GROW IN HIM AND HIS
COMMANDMENTS
AND
COMMISSION

Sometimes we need to see things 'writ large' to get the point.

By crafting the sentence carefully it meant I could give the church just a letter and a number to try and remember. The hope is that in referring to us being a C4 Church it may then prompt the full sentence.

So what is the intention of an aim?

To know what to aim for.

I had known for a while that I wanted to sum up the headship of Jesus, the need for us to commit to him and grow more and more into his likeness to be able to fulfil the Great Commandments and the Great Commission.

I couldn't see what would be missing if a disciple had these qualities:

Acknowledging Jesus as the Christ, our Saviour.

Committing to him and accepting his Lordship.

Working on growing more and more into his likeness.

By doing so, seeing our love of God and of our neighbour flourish.

Our whole life in worship of God, fellowship with other believers and in ministries to others.

And in partnership with the Holy Spirit, going out to the world to introduce people who are far from God, to Jesus and helping them to grow as disciples too.

The Great Commandment and Great Commission hold so much truth for us that acknowledging and following them should bring very real fruit for the Kingdom but having an aim with that long list would never be remembered by the church. C4 is a lot easier to keep in the mind.

I have had some criticism from folk who haven't quite grasped the full concept of C4 Church and think they hear that our only aim is to grow and make disciples. They rightly worry that we could be too church focussed and not offer a compassionate or caring perspective within our local community. However, this is very far from our outcome.

As people grow to become more like Jesus they want to do the things that Jesus did. Mature disciples need to be given freedom to connect with external ministries or maybe start a new one on home turf. If the church helps them by encouraging and feeding in relevant ways, then in releasing them to become the part of the body God has planned for them, the church becomes the body of Christ more fully.

There is a real need to encourage diversity of ministry to enable the body to flourish in the world. (Within the later chapter *"Kitchens"* you will find more on this topic.) Locally to ourselves are many ministries to the disadvantaged and over time we see members of the congregation taking their part in God's Kingdom activity outside the church in the community. And we shouldn't be surprised by this, as when folk start to become more like Jesus they will want to be about the Father's business just as he did.

But C4 is just the aim.

For this simple aim to be owned by everyone they also all need to have an idea of how to put it into practice in the area of church life they are involved in.

So now for the 'how', and this is where it finally gets really simple...

Chapter 7

Gardens, Dining Rooms and Kitchens

It isn't just the aim that needs to be easily remembered by the church community, but also the 'how'. For a body to work, all the parts, everyone in the church, need to know how they fit into the body.

Often disciples want to respond to the prompts God gives them. Maybe they feel led to get a craft group going to help church and non-church folk to mix, or they could equally just have a love for all things Christmas and want to put on the best Carol Service possible. These are great things, but events that on their own won't significantly improve the chances of a guest far from Jesus knowing how to get closer to him.

But what if the individuals who want to put on these events knew how they might fit into a bigger picture and by just tailoring some aspects?

For instance, what if alongside the year round craft programme, there was a December Christmas themed gathering with invites to a Carol Service that was guest friendly? It wouldn't be the first thing thought of by a church person interested in crafts, but if we can all get a framework into the DNA of the church we can begin to think that way, and then we all benefit.

Just to extend this further, what if the Christmas team who now know about the principle of offering something else as an option after their event, can see a need for something they could suggest to people who come to a Carol Service. Maybe in their context they see if someone might run an Alpha Course in January? Then they do some Christmas themed Alpha adverts and flyers and give them out at the Carols evening?

The next step for someone coming out of Alpha would be some sort of small group experience. If that isn't in place and ready before the course, you may bring someone closer to Jesus and then leave them stranded. However, maybe now you are starting to think this way and you could have someone from one of your existing small groups sit in on the course to get to know the guests. Then they can invite some to join their group at the end of the course.

If we all begin to think in terms of what happens before and after what we do and contemplate their place on a journey someone may take, then there can be more opportunities for individuals to grow without church created hiccoughs.

But it needs to be simple if the church community are to grasp the concept and run with it.

Therefore we have just three very basic generic settings to help everyone get a feel for the journey concept of outreach and discipleship growth.

Professional ministers get taught about the many and multiple steps people take in moving from no knowledge of God to an awareness of him, through to discovering and then following Jesus using something like the Engels[8] scale. As an example, it's a well known concept in theological colleges and along with other scales, gives very thorough listings often of more than ten well described various stages in the growth of an individual from non-believer to active believer. While they are undoubtedly close to the truth of how many folk take multiple steps in their journey, they don't really help an ordinary church member to grasp and apply the need to plan for stages or recognise where their ministry fits in. It is just too complicated.

---

[8] James F. Engel What's Gone Wrong With The Harvest, Grand Rapids: Zondervan Press, 1975

That's why we have just three, and it's a picture of domesticity built around food and recognised by most people.

We have *Gardens, Dining Rooms and Kitchens* and in the *Kitchen* we have a *Sink* and an *Oven* with a back door to again reach guests in the *Garden*. That's it. A simple domestic recognisable analogy for a church, complete with all its outreach and discipleship. Three well recognised and memorable spaces with two kitchen items that all tie together in an analogy we all get - how we might eat with a guest, a friend or a family member in our own home.

At my first evening gathering in Plymouth I moved from the C4 aim into the 'how'. The theology of 'why' is summed up in the statement that we would want to be a church that is about "Christ and our Commitment to grow in him and his Commandments and Commission", but that aim doesn't tell anyone how you might achieve it together. So we looked at the 'how'.

We had a BBQ on one side to illustrate the *Garden*, a laid out dining table in the middle with a white table cloth, silver cutlery and candlesticks for the *Dining Room* and on the other side a simple bare table with an open milk carton, ketchup bottle and mugs for the *Kitchen* and we thought about food, including the washing up and its preparation.

These are settings folk know. We then talked about how people interact in the different settings and how they generally eat with their family or how they might with invited guests or friends.

For instance, if someone doesn't know you or other people well, they are more like a guest than a friend and a good question we would probably ask ourselves is, 'what type of meal we might invite them to in our own home?' Are they more likely to come to an open BBQ in the *Garden* where they can arrive and leave easily and hide in a larger crowd? Or to a formal smaller and more intimate dinner party with folk they don't know and can't easily leave if they don't feel comfortable? A guest is more likely to prefer the BBQ in the *Garden*.

But if they were nearly your friend and you wanted to introduce them to some of your other friends they may by now have already heard about, wouldn't a smaller setting in a *Dining Room* with a few selected folk be better where friendships could be encouraged more?

The last room is for those folk who are your family, the place where most family food is often prepared and consumed, the *Kitchen*.

We don't worry about table cloths or matching cutlery in the *Kitchen*. We probably leave the ketchup out for the meal. We might also go through what each of us have been doing that day, or will be doing, while we're preparing the food and eating it. We conduct family business in the *Kitchen*. Hopefully as family we also help with the washing up at the *Sink* and maybe we would have joined in with cooking the food as well at the *Oven*.

A little later on, after we had used the set in church of the tables and a BBQ, I asked a good friend in our church who was an architect, if he might be able to produce a walk through video of a house for me to help explain it without needing to build a small set for the three different settings.

I wanted to arrive at the driveway and come into the *Garden* where it was set up for a BBQ and pause while being able to see the patio doors into the *Dining Room* of the house so I could talk about *Gardens*. I wanted us to see the *Dining Room* was visible from the *Garden* and then move into it through the glazed doors. It is set out ready, and we can pause again to chat about what type of church events might suit these settings, while seeing the open *Kitchen* door ahead. After a short stay, the video then goes through that door into the *Kitchen* where the table sits. Again a short pause and more chat and the view turns to see the *Sink* and ministries are talked about, before looking at the *Oven* to mention mission, and finally turning to go out the back door into the *Garden* again to meet the guests.

The images you see on these pages and the front cover are from that video and it really helped set the scene for our teaching on the topic. *(If you would like a copy of the video you can download it for free from http://www.judes.org.uk/explosive-mission/)*

If you decide to use some of the ideas from this book in your own church, feel free to use the video and explain the concept to a group of folk. They can then easily see the whole journey in a memorable way, as a metaphor for the invitation and walk towards Jesus, getting to become part of his family and then taking our part in the family, before going back out the rear door into the *Garden* to meet other new people coming in.

It is far more easily remembered that a ten step academic principle of how people change in their relationship to God, and far simpler for the church to take on board as a whole strategy.

So, the settings of the three spaces need to suit each type of person we are able to reach and they need to be suitable for them in their walk. Each person needs to be able to see the next room's opportunities so that they can decide to move in closer in their own time. People may stay in *Garden* settings for years, so we need a lot of variety for them. Over time they should begin to realise that they are welcome guests, that we can be trusted and that there is more available for them if they want to move forward.

These settings are crucial for the important action of the Holy Spirit in drawing people closer to Jesus. It might be that we need to wait for his timing in asking someone to something as a next step. If it is his timing it will strike home at their heart and they will know it makes good sense. Of course the decision is still theirs, and if we operate in this way, always open to the Spirit's gentle prompt at some point, then we shall avoid being pushy and still have the greatest opportunity to share the hope we have.

By recognising the action of the Holy Spirit we can then put our energy and resources into providing the best environment for him to meet people. However, if we host guests at something reminiscent of a 1970's church tea in a cold hall that hasn't been decorated since the war, instead of a friendly well decorated, warm venue with soft seating and pleasant music, and good quality food, maybe we aren't doing our bit?

But, if we openly and honestly show that we value people then we help them to be open to the Holy Spirit's prompt. We do know how to provide the right environment or setting for each group of people, young or old, close to or far from Christ, because we do it outside the church setting in our own local social setting. We just need to keep this in mind as we plan an event. Is it for a guest, or a friend, or a family member? Then we can convert our thoughts into the planning and provision of our events, remembering they must also offer a connection from a prior stage or to a next step.

Each mix of people will have different needs and we need the sensitivity to make them as comfortable as we can at each step of their walk. It helps to remember that we can't influence anyone's heart. All we can provide are the best and most suitable environments for each person, young or old, as partners with our God of mission.

That is the general description of *Gardens, Dining Rooms and Kitchens*. Now for a bit more detail...

Chapter 8

The Garden

Garden settings are all about the Guest.

Consider how you might prepare for a crowd of twenty or thirty people coming for a BBQ in your own garden at home. What sort of things might you do? Maybe buy good food that can be eaten while standing and take time preparing it. You might mow the lawn and tidy up the garden and put the kids' toys away. You may even decorate the outside a bit with some lights or garden flares.

Then, as the time approaches, you have a shower and get dressed in relaxed but smart clothes to suit the event and the rest of the family are encouraged to do the same. One of them can be near the garden gate to welcome folk as they arrive, someone else gets them a drink and you introduce them to other guests and encourage the conversations.

And the conversations in the *Garden* are light hearted. As an example, if you were at home you wouldn't tell a guest about your Uncle's drinking problem or your child's struggle with a neighbour's child at school. You don't talk about family problems at gatherings like these, so why start when we do it for the church?

And that's the way to treat *Garden* settings: create them with the same heart you would at home, keeping in your mind the thought that you are entertaining a guest, and ensure at all times that they feel welcome.

These settings are all about the guest, not your church members. If that is your team's mindset as they create the event it should come easily. For instance, it could be an inexpensive quiz night with some simple food and questions suitable for everyone. You can choose a local venue not in the church, maybe somewhere with a bar, then you can begin to make people comfortable and help them to feel welcomed. And don't talk about 'family' problems, how you view baptism differently from the church down the road, or that you can't believe the Pastor at the other church wears vestments (or doesn't, depending on your churchmanship), don't criticise your Youth Worker or speak about how that chap with the hygiene issues sat next to you last weekend. They are guests, not family.

A *Garden* setting shouldn't be challenging and you may not even see the Gospel obviously within it. It is about the starting point of a relationship and it needs to be genuine.

There is nothing wrong about having a Harvest Barn Dance, with church members inviting friends and them all having a good time. It's a good thing in itself. It also shows non-church folk we don't have two heads even if we do have two left feet! We can show just how normal and fun loving we are at events like this. It often comes as a surprise to guests when they see we do enjoy life, we don't do glum or boring things and that we do know how to smile and not be condescending or judgemental.

However, the strategic planning also needs to let our guests see there is something they can do to become part of what they are witnessing, maybe as simple as a flyer for another event or a taster evening for an Alpha Course, or the various festival services such as Mother's Day, Easter, Harvest or Christmas. These are just small steps towards the Kingdom in easily identifiable ways and this is easy outreach, but it is also easy to forget to plan for, or recognise what might already be in existence, a next step. So if you were to use the Harvest Barn Dance as an example, do it before your Harvest services, not after. Then you have something you can invite guests to!

You must ensure your guests know it exists and that they would be welcomed if they wanted to come. If you don't tell them it is available, all you have done is given them a fun time out and you have reduced the opportunity from all your hard work to bring someone a step closer to Jesus.

Of course, we don't always have to create a follow on *Dining Room* setting as it might already exist. The *Garden* events are often the easiest to create, but there can be a danger in a church with restricted resources of putting a huge effort into lots of them with no result for the Kingdom if they aren't strategically planned into a whole church outreach and discipleship framework like *Gardens, Dining Rooms and Kitchens*.

As a further example, if you know you will have a very friendly guest focused event in Church on Mother's Day, then you could organise your quiz night for a week or two beforehand and achieve a greater potential from the same amount of organising. Consider if the Quiz Night were in late January, but there is nothing soon in the church diary following it suitable for a guest. You either waste an opportunity or you have to create a second event to follow the first. But the alternative if you begin to think this way is just moving the Quiz Night to a fortnight before Mother's Day. It is only an example, but it illustrates how being a little bit smarter can give a greater opportunity to your guest to begin to discover Jesus.

These things may not always work, but trying is a good thing and we learn from mistakes. An example of trying something like the Quiz Night idea, but not quite getting it right relates to our church's Boys' and Girls' Brigades. St Jude's has been a family relevant church for more than a century. Our Boys' Brigade began in 1902, five years before Baden-Powell started the Scouts. The Brigades are similarly uniformed groups for kids from 5 to 18 and on into leadership roles after 18 but with a Christian ethos and teaching. They fit well as an option for some of our local children.

We could see the Brigades were brilliant at including new kids when they came along but they didn't really have a *Garden* setting where children could come and taste without feeling any pressure to join, other than coming along to a normal evening. So the age old favourite of a summer holiday club seemed a great idea. We could have a week of lots of activities that reflected what happens on the Brigade evenings. The children could have a great time for part of their summer holidays and we would then end by saying if they want to do this more, then they can come and try our Brigade evenings. This is a good example of an invitation from the *Garden* to the *Dining Room* for children.

We have already mentioned shifting the timing of existing ministries to work better and we tried that for this Holiday Club. Most local summer groups happen at the beginning of the school holidays, flyers go into schools in the last week and the kids come along the following week. But if we did that, the Brigades wouldn't be starting back up for their new term for about six weeks, by which time the memory of the fun will have diminished. So we thought strategically. We had our Summer Holiday Club the last full week of the school holidays so there would just be two weeks before the Brigades began. But, a significant problem we had was it was about 6 weeks after the schools closed and our publicity wasn't remembered, and only a very small number came along.

The principle was right, but the promotion was poor. Next time we'll have big banners up throughout the summer holidays to back up the flyers at the beginning.

So even though it didn't work, we know the reason for the timing was right and we'll undoubtedly come back to it again with a tweak or two when we get our resources lined up. I mention it because it reinforces the principle of a *Garden* event for a particular segment of the surrounding community, as an easily accessible setting suitable for a particular group of guests that has an embedded well signposted next step to a *Dining Room.*

I also mention it to show we haven't got it all right either. We still have lots of gaps in our provision, but maybe the difference is that we know where the gaps are.

And this is where we now move, from the *Garden* to the *Dining Room.*

.

Chapter 9

The Dining Room

Dining Rooms are where friends eat. Intimate dinners with a smaller group of folk gathered around in a setting that encourages the building of friendships.

That's what the *Dining Room* is about, friends.

We started the *Garden* concept by asking how you might arrange a large BBQ. So now, how instead might you arrange an intimate dinner for 6 or 8 people you want to build your friendship with?

You already know these people a little, but they might not yet know everyone at the table. Again you will take time in planning and making sure you will help them to feel welcome. You could consider giving them a formal invitation because it is important for you to know the seating plan or because the food you will prepare will be expensive. Along with wanting it all to work smoothly, you also want them to feel special by giving them this invitation. At the same time you might ask about any dietary needs, because they need to know you care about them. You try and avoid being out of the room too much, so you plan your menu carefully because it is about good conversation over the lovely food you will make.

As you know a little about everyone's background as the host, you can introduce topics and have deeper conversations that will help everyone get closer to each other. Evenings like this can easily begin to form whole new friendships between people who didn't know each other much before.

And when folk leave, the regular phrase of "We must do this again" often arises. Absolutely!

That is what we would do at home and again, when we come to think of something for the same purpose within a church, we need the same mindset. Also, remember that these settings require closer attention and are harder to get right. They need to be tailored to the smaller cohort of guests so that they might become friends of yours and of the other guests. The *Dining Room* is about building closer relationships and the people from the church who will be hosts need to know, and be suitable to make these closer connections. That may mean they will become involved in the lives of the guests who will hopefully become friends.

All we do should also be about reality and honesty. There is a danger that we see people who aren't in the church as 'targets' for conversion. But that isn't God's perspective at all, so it shouldn't be ours. We know we are called to love people and introduce them to Jesus. I have always strived to avoid being in a situation where I may struggle if I'm asked the following question by someone: 'Are you friendly with me because you want to convert me or do you want to help me make this decision because you are my friend?' It is an uncomfortable place if you can't answer that correctly.

So again, folk might dwell in this area for some time, but always need to be able to see through the *Kitchen* door into the family space.

There would be the photos on the fridge door and the noise of the rest of the family working together to get the food ready. They might begin to experience the impact of a close family co-operating who want their guest to become a friend and hopefully, eventually, become a part of their extended family.

You can begin to imagine how this works at home, but how do you do it in a church setting?

You have got to know a few folk and they might know one or two others. But what might you arrange to enable longer chats, over which they can get to know each other and others you introduce them to from the church family?

In many ways this is the hardest stage to arrange and it requires a greater investment in time because you want these guests to become friends. Some of the evangelistic courses can work well here, courses like Alpha or Christianity Explored. But you need to put in the effort to make your guests comfortable enough to become friends.

One of our small groups who meet in a home had regular social events as a group. This means their non-church gatherings are smaller than a big church and the conversations can be longer. Sometimes they just get the guys together to watch an action movie or go out for a curry. The women liked reading varied novels so they formed a book reading club and invited mums from the school gate to join them. Because they met fairly regularly, friendships could evolve quite naturally. And of course, they had a built in *Kitchen* opportunity because their social events came out of it, their own small group. If their guests became friends and wanted to spend more time with this new group they could always join them for their weekly small group and become a part of the family.

However, we need to keep in our minds that close friendship with us isn't what Jesus asked us to do. These relationships with new people do need to be genuine, but ultimately Jesus wants everyone to be in his family, not just ours.

So when we do these things we need to keep the same principle in mind. We need to ensure that some sort of small next step is obvious in case someone wants to make a step from the *Dining Room* towards the *Kitchen* and join the family.

Chapter 10

The Kitchen

Kitchens are places where families eat.

Cooking for 50 guests and helping them all to something to eat is what a BBQ in the *Garden* is for, not the *Kitchen.*

Similarly, getting the silver out, ironing the napkins and tablecloth, planning three balanced and interesting courses of beautifully presented food every day is a chore beyond any normal and sane family. No rational family eats that way. Instead, milk bottles are on the table at breakfast, lunch is a sandwich rushed and shared, and dinner is a stew in a bowl and a pot of yoghurt from the fridge. Well it is in my house and it often happens in the *Kitchen*. Life happens here.

In the *Kitchen* conversations are about our daily lives. Thinks like, what was school like, how was the working day, who is in and who is going out and what lifts are needed? Problems at school are chatted about and difficulties with the neighbour or Aunty Ethel. The lack of money at the end of the month will undoubtedly crop up in most homes too.

These are ordinary family conversations.

And the family is the right place to deal with these. We don't burden our friends with this sort of stuff and we definitely wouldn't talk about our household budget difficulties with a guest at a BBQ, so we shouldn't do it in a church context when guests are present.

When one of the family is struggling, maybe homework is tough this week, then the parents or an older sibling lend a hand. When someone's had an achievement, you might decide to celebrate and go out for a meal or bring in a take-away.

When the kids are growing we show them new skills such as how to make a cup of tea or boil an egg or maybe make some porridge or an omelette. So, when a new Christian joins a group, we can help them in similar ways to enable them to grow as disciples, for instance ways of reading the Bible or exploring prayer to make it more fulfilling.

And if the family have a 'big do' coming up, like Christmas, when you might invite some friends and neighbours to come round, you all work together and assign roles and get welcoming. Some will do what they can and others will do more. The six year old might not be able to make the mince pies but they can look really cute with a plate going round offering them!

We know how to do it in our homes and this is how the church family should operate, with close fellowship where we help each other grow as disciples, encourage each other in ministries, celebrate and worship together in suitable ways and work together to find ways we can all be involved with mission.

I mentioned in the chapter on 'The Aim: C4 Church' that some folk have misheard when it has been mentioned the focus is on mission and discipleship. Often their concern is that ministries to the hurting in our communities might be left out and that there is a danger we become too church focused.

But we needn't get worried about this reasonable concern because the 'family' units of the church in the *Kitchen* settings are crucial in enabling folk to grow into fully rounded disciples. As they grow, they will want to be a part of some sort of ministry to the poor and disenfranchised, the ill and the lonely. It can happen quite naturally in ways that God may plan, as parts of the body become stronger and work together.

And as we know, the 'Body of Christ' image for the church is one of diversity. We don't all need to be the same. It works better if we are encouraged to be different and work to our strengths. A knee works really well if it recognises it isn't a foot and follows the specific signals the brain sends it and doesn't pick up on the ones sent to the foot!

In the same way we may need to find a way of encouraging any small groups to be different and not alike. For many churches the small group, or cell, or cluster, or home group (we have so many names for these gatherings!) are a vital part of our health and they need to discover their own identity and purposes. We need lots of different *Kitchen* settings.

As an example of encouraging diversity, within my own church we used an analogy to reflect the role of the church alongside small groups and their function. It is based on an acrostic of the UK coastal rescue service, the Royal National Lifeboat Institution, or RNLI.

The primary function of the RNLI is lifesaving. The obvious similarity to the church is Jesus' instruction to offer the saving hand to those that are lost on the seas of life.

We also saw a similarity in the organisational structure of the RNLI that could help us. Their HQ in Poole, Dorset, trains, resources and supports a multitude of different lifesaving groups around the shores of the UK such as deep sea life boats, inshore fast semi-inflatable craft and beach teams with surf boards and swimmers with floats.

Our main church functions in a similar way.

The central organisation, courses and main Sunday services often exist to enable and support our churchgoers in their everyday life. They provide an opportunity for the larger crowd to gather for celebration or teaching in ways that can't be replicated in a small group setting. However the large setting isn't best suited to save individuals. Just as the RNLI doesn't send out lifeboats from its HQ, but different ones from different locations, so the church is faced with the same issue.

We recognised a need to co-operate in smaller clusters of people. Those folk needed to find their own expression as a group as they may be very different to another, just as a deep sea lifeboat team will vary greatly from a beach team with surfboards. And that expression might not just be around meeting for fellowship or prayer or worship, it might be to perform some sort of ministry or outreach at times.

We can get fixated on what God wants of each of us and often, when we read scripture we personalise it as we reflect upon a verse. "What might this mean for me?" could be a common thread of thought for us. But as I looked at Paul's letters to the churches I realised they are written to churches.

"Duh", you may well say!

But the implication was so stark for me on how our small groups could be quite crucial in the health of the church.

As an example, consider Ephesians 2:10

For we are God's workmanship, created in Christ Jesus to do good works, which God prepared in advance for us to do.

The thing is, Paul isn't writing to an individual, but to a community in Ephesus. As individuals we can reflect on these words and think, 'Well, I have a ministry of good works to discover…'. Instead, maybe we need to think of a group of people needing to discover the 'good works' God has planned for them?

In a similar vein, how might we re-read the following passages of Paul:

To the church in Philippi (1:27):

"contend as one man for the faith of the gospel"

Or to the church in Colossae (4:5-6)

"Be wise in the way you act towards outsiders; make the most of every opportunity"

By encouraging folk to collect together regularly in smaller groups we can take passages such as these and consider how we might put them more fully into practice as a small group of people in ways a large Sunday gathering or an individual never could.

Therefore, the ministries to the disenfranchised or hurting don't get missed by concentrating on making disciples, because that is what disciples want to do.

So an important part of this was also to encourage each group to form its own identity, its own DNA around their own shape. They needed to discover what they naturally felt drawn to do together.

These small groups have the potential to be the power houses of our churches as within them we can see close meaningful fellowship and accountable, confidential discipleship. They are perfect *Kitchens* for adults.

As individuals and the group grow to become more like Jesus, they will want to do what Jesus did. They will encourage each other to do something, and possibly do it together. If an individual wants to join a ministry external to them, they can, as a group, help them in that decision. That may be to the homeless or to assist those in debt perhaps, but they will always have a small group to still hear their news and woes, to pray for them and help them maintain their 'good works'.

And so we modified the letters of the RNLI for our own acrostic for Rescuing, Nurturing, Loving and Including – all great features for groups to aspire to within a context of rescue.

Rescuing
Nurturing
Loving
Including

small group
CHURCH

These are a wonderful *Kitchen* aims. A place where the family gathers, where ties are strengthened and we minister to each other's needs as they arise. Difficult life decisions can be shared and Bible perspectives encouraged as we grow as disciples. Maybe as a group there could be some social occasions when friends can be invited, a small group's own *Garden* event, like the film nights or book club as mentioned earlier.

And worship can be so much more meaningful in a small group. Maybe to help think about this aspect of the group we can take one last look at Paul's letters, this time to do with gathered worship from his letter to Colossae (3:16).

As you read it, consider again who Paul is writing to, a group of people who probably met in a house. I would suggest this is a group bigger than 2 or 3 but smaller than 100...

"Let the words of Christ dwell in you richly as you teach and admonish one another with all wisdom, and as you sing psalms, hymns and spiritual songs with gratitude in your hearts to God"

Why do I suggest this group bigger than 2 or 3 and smaller than 100?

It is not to do with the fact that the church Paul wrote to probably met in a home and that it would have been an unusual house to have been large enough to include 100 folk. Instead, it is difficult to 'admonish' pastorally within a crowd of 100 and equally really hard to sing when there are just two or three gathered. Maybe the family unit of a small group, a *Kitchen* setting, is the answer?

We still often need the larger gatherings for mutual support and maybe some extra teaching and resourcing, but these groups can achieve a lot on their own, particularly in encouraging and growing disciples. Just like the RNLI needs an HQ, a church needs a larger gathering, but the outward effect of the organisation can come more effectively from the smaller group.

And so, with a safe place to have fellowship with others, we come to look a bit more closely at some discipleship issues. This might be to encourage individuals into a ministry at a stage that suits them, and to help them take part in mission in a way that will match their character.

Therefore, the *Kitchen* within this framework model has two specific parts picked out to ensure we don't miss them off the list of things to help people grow in our desire to fulfil the Great Commission of raising disciples. They are the *Sink* and the *Oven*.

These are the parts it would be easy to miss if this was just a missional model, but we saw earlier that having a planned growth route for new churchgoers is crucial or they may in time be happy to stay being fed, stop growing and instead just get spiritually overweight. We also discovered that it's a significant part of the answer to the conundrum we have at the heart of this book:

> *While we may 'do' outreach, it is the Holy Spirit who encourages someone towards a church so they can both encounter Jesus **and** grow in Him. If the church can't offer that discipleship, why would the Holy Spirit bring them?*

So we know that overfeeding people Bible knowledge and not encouraging them further is not what Jesus asked us to do. He asked us in the Great Commission to teach them everything he has taught us. (Matthew 28:20) That includes ministries of love for others, as real love is based in actions not feelings.

Therefore, the first of the two areas within the *Kitchen* is the *Sink…*

Chapter 11

The Sink

When families get together for a meal in the kitchen, it soon becomes apparent that there is a job to do that in the end needs to be shared to avoid family stress, the washing up.

At home we might not get our 5 year olds to do it, but by the time they are teenagers we get frustrated if they don't at least put the dishes in the sink or the dishwasher! As our children grow we all start to encourage them in doing their part and we all know the conflicts that can arise when they don't.

It is so often said about churches that 80% of the work is done by 20% of the people. But that can't be right, can it? It is very much like the often quoted observation that churches are like football matches where there are 22 people exercising and needing a rest, being watched by 22,000 people resting, desperately in need of exercise.

Do we really just want to accept that situation?

We know the Bible strongly recommends that God has got things for us to do: we have already looked at Jesus speaking of the need for the 'workers in the vineyard'. And group sanity also requires we encourage people to do their bit. If we don't help newer people into ministries we will also stress out our most committed. But it isn't really about our churches getting things done, that's just a nice by-product. This is about helping people to grow to become more like Christ, growing as disciples.

So the *Sink* is a really important part of the framework of *Gardens, Dining Rooms and Kitchens*. If we want to grow rounded disciples we will need to help them to discover their ministry within the community and maybe outside it too.

Often we think of a ministry as something we do for our church, but it can also be a service we give to others outside our faith community, fulfilling St Francis' idea to 'preach the Gospel, and if necessary, use words'.

I wouldn't want to get hung up on the specific meaning of a word like 'ministry', but a significant part of its meaning is what we do inside the church for the church community. It may be easier to think that there will always be a role, or roles, for each of us within our churches and that some of us may also have one outside, in the area we live, that is also missional.

But notice where the *Sink* is, it's in the *Kitchen.*

We don't ask guests to tidy up after the BBQ or suggest to friends that they might like to do the dishes after a dinner party. That is what the family does. The church should be the same. As we become part of the family, we should pick up our own share of the chores, to be fair to everyone else and to help us all grow to become more like our servant King.

If we are to pick up again on the 'body' image, we need to find out which part of the body we are. We looked earlier at Ephesians 2:10 that says:

For we are God's workmanship, created in Christ Jesus to do good works, which God prepared in advance for us to do.

The Church may well need to help folk discover what it is that God is getting them ready for.

There can be varied ways of helping folk, maybe with lists of roles that are unfilled or that need support so they can look and see what may suit them best. Maybe better would be a course based around something like the S.H.A.P.E.[9] principle which suggests that God has 'shaped' each of us for a purpose and we can help each person to search for their own shape.

---

[9] 2002 Rick Warren *The Purpose-Driven Life* Zondervan pg 236

The recognition behind this search is that square pegs can't fit into, don't like, or won't stay long in a round hole. But when that space is your shape you both fit in and are passionate about it because it is what God has gifted you for spiritually and it drives your heart's passions. Those skills you have built up give you the right mix of abilities and the method of delivery suits your personality. Finally, all your life experiences can come into play and you can discover that your personality is suited to it.

What type of teaching could you offer your folk?

It undoubtedly will need to help them think through what God would like them to do in His Kingdom which he had prepared in advance for them to do.

This is where the *Gardens, Dining Room and Kitchen* framework really comes into play for each sector of person joining your church. At some point, have you got a plan for how you might help them discover their ministry?

As an example, when we set up our renewed Sunday morning 'Kids' Church' alongside our adult service, we tried to have opportunities for the teenagers to be able to be a part of the provision. As someone else said, 'children aren't disciples in waiting, they are disciples in training'. The teenagers are discovering ministry alongside the adult leaders.

But a balanced Christian would not just be a worshipper of God through their lives and be together with others in fellowship, becoming a growing disciple with a ministry. We still need one more string to our bow to be the full human being God planned us to be. We all need to know our place of partnership in God's mission to his world.

Hence, the *Oven...*

Chapter 12

The Oven

In the *Kitchen*, things get finished at the *Oven*.

So far we have looked at enabling people in their walk. Trying to help them live lives that worship God as well as creating community to enable fellowship and discipleship opportunities. In the last chapter we looked at encouraging folk in discovering the ministry that matches their shape. And now we come to discovering our place in mission.

We can help individuals discover their mission strengths.

It might be how they can bring the gospel to their friends and acquaintances, possibly using some church co-ordinated *Garden* events. Maybe for some it will be a discovery that fields further from home might be their calling.

And then for some, while going through a discovery process at the *Sink* they may start to think of their ministry task as mission, and that is great. For an individual to discover that God is building them up ready for work within his Kingdom in some sort of missionary role is exciting. But he doesn't call most people to a mission field overseas, so there is no need to panic!

While being an evangelist is quite possible, we know that only some are called to be that and are given that spiritual gift (Ephesians 4:11). But we are all asked to be witnesses. In fact in 1 Peter 3:15-16 we are called upon to …

Always be prepared to give an answer to everyone who asks you to give the reason for the hope that you have. But do this with gentleness and respect

And so, finally, there is a need for something within our *Gardens, Dining Rooms and Kitchens* framework to help people discover how to fulfil this call to be prepared for mission.

For this part of our adult framework we found a great resource[10] that fits well into our overall framework of guests, friends and family and suits everyone here as well as our framework strategy.

---

[10] 2006 Bill Hybels *"Just walk across the room."* (Zondervan)

You may well find your own, but I can explain a bit about what we have used. The principle is making friends and acquaintances. Not that hard so far. Then you keep them as friends, which is fairly normal still. But, you also acknowledge that at some time in that friendship God may prompt you through the Holy Spirit to say or do something. It might be within the first few months, it might be 10 years down the line, but it will be at the right time. It requires us to acknowledge and to listen for the Holy Spirit's prompting, but we have already seen the need to recognise the shepherd's voice.

I am sure you can find something to suit your situation to help individuals begin in mission. Maybe as a start it could simply be to introduce them to the missional principles of *Gardens, Dining Rooms and Kitchens.*

And while we're at this point, just an observation about using courses written and produced by others.

I have never really understood why some churches don't use what can be a high quality, well produced resource from some of the larger churches around the world, especially in smaller churches where resources are tight. We had touched briefly earlier how some churches can expect their leaders to be multi-disciplined experts who can work 80 hour weeks while helping their spouses and family thrive. However, expecting them to also re-invent the wheel and produce wonderful and professional independent courses for all your church's needs, when you have no staff and are overworked just isn't going to happen most of the time.

When you're a smaller church it isn't a bad idea to get into the habit of using someone else's materials. I sometimes think the pressure to be superhuman means some pastors don't feel they should present a video course. But if there is a great one available, do we really expect our own home grown team to both replicate the material and the quality? I remember the reaction folk had to Nicky Gumbel in the early Alpha Course videos. He is a well educated and erudite chap based in wealthy West London with a congregation that is younger and more prosperous than many of our churches. Because it was the first time many had been exposed to video teaching, some couldn't get past the conflict of cultures when they saw his congregation and heard his accent.

In more recent years I remember some people having a real problem with Rick Warren's bright shirts on his DVD's. It was predominantly because they began with a view based on a stereotype the British have of Californians. For some this made listening to him difficult because they couldn't get past his Hawaiian shirts or his laughing at his own jokes. But, after a couple of occasions and use of these types of curriculum, my own congregation don't react the same way anymore and can listen to the messages of others more easily, though I still get comments about the wonderful locations and sunny weather that always seems to be on these DVD's compared to our own weather. So my recommendation when it comes to thinking about using a DVD based course from elsewhere, when you're restricted in your options, is to seriously consider using them.

Also, do you remember an early intention of this strategy is to increase the workers in the vineyard? Well, another benefit of these previously prepared courses is that they don't need a qualified and theologically trained church leader to present them to a church or small group. If the content is sound and suits your need they can be delivered by a competent member of your congregation.

We have started to realise that some of the courses we have used over the years in our small groups can help in our strategy if we used them semi-regularly. But we can't ask a small group to repetitively use the same material for the odd new member.

We can see a gap in our provision when we put the *Gardens, Dining Room and Kitchens* framework on our own church and we know we need to find an alternative away to help our newest church members other than just expecting the small groups to pick up the role.

Consider the new person joining your church. They aren't going to get the church's 'basics' in a small group if they join one after the group has already done it. You can't keep teaching the topic on Sunday mornings or your regular congregation will leave. So it does need a venue to give a new person some background to your church and for the other courses for the *Sink* and *Oven*.

Maybe as a starting point it would be helpful to offer a 'welcome to the family' module that you build yourself to suit your context.

Ideally using a midweek evening will suit people, but today, taking out time for many people with yet another evening is limited as folk get busier, so we are also looking at the time we know they are coming, Sunday mornings. We may not do it, but this is such an important need we will think outside the normal box if it is needed.

So whether it is an evening or a Sunday morning class like one of our new *Kitchens,* they will be a little more like one the army might put up, a field *Kitchen,* temporary and focused for a purpose. They could be for a welcome course that extends into material on how to become a well balanced disciple within our church. A second will undoubtedly be our 'Discovering Your Ministry' course, a spell at the *Sink.* And we will want to offer something to give them encouragement in being involved in mission, a course while at the *Oven.* The small groups can achieve a lot in these areas, but we expect they need help from outside.

This is what we're doing or planning in our own context. I don't want to suggest you use the same materials. What I do hope is that you can now start to see a need and a space to be able to bring your own churchmanship needs before someone new. There are a lot of varied resources available out there. How might you do that where you are?

Chapter 13

Back to the Garden

The work of the *Kitchen* will continue for all of us throughout our lives, as we live in the family of God and grow more and more towards the likeness of Jesus together with our brothers and sisters.

But we aren't made to stay in the *Kitchen* with our church family all the time. Of the many things we can do on earth, mission is the one thing we need to get better at now. So much of who we are only gets perfected as we leave this life and start our eternal one, but mission is one thing we will have no need of later. Therefore we don't really have an excuse for putting it off any more. While in glory we will definitely worship our God and spend time with the other saints: maybe we will even have evolving roles and service to them and our Creator, after all we're going to be there for eternity. But one thing is fairly certain, there will be no need to reach the lost.

So we do need to encourage our people to pass out of the *Kitchen* door and back into the *Garden* this side of eternity. But remember, the *Garden* has to suit the guests.

This may seem obvious and it has been stated earlier, but we must ensure the things we might invite folk to are of a quality that is suitable for a guest. Too many of our churches put on events that are based on church culture and not the culture of those we would like to meet. If we keep on doing that, our people will just stop inviting any acquaintances they might have because they don't want to lose them as a friend by embarrassing them.

For many of our church members the *Garden* will be their main place of mission.

As they encourage their own friendships outside the church community there will come a time when they can invite their friend to a church organised event. Maybe instead they will be an organiser and enjoy putting on these types of events, which is in itself a ministry and a missionary activity. Alternatively they might not be involved in networks or situations where they can make friends to invite, but they could be good at mixing with new people they don't know and just chat with them.

Whichever of these or other roles within a *Garden* setting, we do need to be involved in some way. As we discover our gifting and calling for mission, it is important we take it up. Our lives as disciples of Jesus require us to "go and make disciples", not sit and wait.

Maybe as our churches take on board the understanding of a strategy based on guests, friends and family we can get better in our welcoming of guests in all we do and regularly take up our position in the *Garden* as we represent Jesus and his family.

And so, the analogy of the church in operation as it reaches out and makes disciples can be simply summed up in the three rooms and two appliances of the *Garden, Dining Room* and *Kitchen* with its *Sink* and *Oven*, but please, after all that, don't forget the back door to go into the *Garden* once more!

Chapter 14

Some examples in practice

I find church books that unfold programs to be copied out of context into different cultures really frustrating because they often don't translate into our local churches. Hopefully, this volume's focus on a framework instead of a series of programs won't do that for you.

My desire as you have read through this book is that you have found a framework that can fit over your church in your place to help you strategically explore what may be needed for your time, to suit your people, your current size and your resources.

But equally, some examples of how we put this into practice in an ordinary church might show how relatively simple the process is and how, by thinking strategically with a simplified outreach and discipleship model, obvious gaps do become apparent. And remember, these aren't programmes or projects from a mega-church somewhere, just an average sized church with maybe 120 people on a Sunday from kids to elderly. They aren't offered for you to copy, though please feel free to do so if they might work for you. I offer them instead to help explain how this framework strategy has been put into practice.

Even now, writing 'thinking strategically' feels unusual in a church environment, but without doing so we will waste effort, when for many of us our resources are light.

So here are just one or two simple things we did because we have this framework evolving in our church's DNA.

Example 1 Parents & Toddlers

A lot of churches operate drop-in zones for parents and carers to bring along their pre-school children. This is a great aspiration within our communities and brings a much needed place of friendship for many young parents who can often feel isolated. And while it is inherently a good thing to do, too often we will also have a nebulous thought that we might build friendships that mean we can invite someone to come to church. That may be true for some eventually, but there can be another option that is a little more strategic.

These are classic *Garden* settings. It would be great to think we could offer these young parents or carers a tailored Alpha Course with a crèche, but that would be a step too far for many. Therefore we knew we needed an intermediate step, a *Dining Room* where closer friendships could form that was suitable and have directions built in towards an Alpha Course. So we looked for a parenting course based around watching a DVD followed by conversation. Why that way in particular? Well, it allowed friendships to evolve more over some coffee and muffins in a smaller more intimate setting and importantly we were thinking of the next signposted offering. At the end of this course we were able to say, "If you have liked this, would you like to do another similar one with a DVD and chat, this time about Christianity? It's called Alpha".

Of about 30 carers who come each Monday morning with their kids to the drop-in, about 8 came to the parenting course with a creche. Half of those came to an Alpha Course, three joined a small group who hadn't been churchgoers before, and one asked to be baptised. That was a great afternoon out for a large group of us on the beach after the Sunday morning services. In this case a completed movement from a guest, to becoming a friend, and evolved into joining the family.

Example 2 Kids

We had a Nativity service with our Pre-School children, an evening Carol service, a Midnight Christmas Eve Communion and Christmas Day gatherings, but strangely we discovered as we looked at our provision that we missed our major area of contact at Christmas – families. You might think that odd from this list, but when I laid the framework over what we did, there was this obvious gap.

Eight year olds don't like an hour of carols that might go on until 8pm, midnight Christmas Eve patently isn't an option and un-churched folk don't normally come out on Christmas Day. But people do want to gather at Christmas with their kids. We needed a *Garden* setting that would suit kids from about 6 to 14 years of age with their parents, complete with directions for next step opportunities. and use the huge draw of Christmas.

Therefore we commissioned a new service led by our Youth and Children's Minister. We didn't want it to be a 'crib service' that 3 and 4 year olds might engage with which, if we are brutally honest, are often really for the Grandparents. We had that opportunity with our Pre-School Nativity. This was to definitely be for the kids, incorporating games and even a voting system each time a song came up.

However, we didn't just want this to be about a Christmas gathering. It started from a realisation that we didn't have one for this age group, but as we have already said, we don't want to just do this one thing when we may be able to achieve more. What could it be a stepping stone for?

We did have settings already for young people to continue a relationship with Jesus. Therefore, we also had adverts and flyers for the Brigades and Youth groups that began again early in January. And so, at 4pm on Christmas Eve, we held our Family Christmas gathering. Families could get their last minute shopping done and then come out to get into the 'Christmas mood', and kids were also offered a chance to join in with groups where they could begin a whole new chapter in their lives. It didn't really cost anything extra to offer it, but the potential for the kids was increased significantly.

It is so easy to forget the next steps to follow any event but after a while you start to think that way whenever you think about a new one.

Example 3 Teenagers

We also spotted a gap in our outreach to teenagers who may not be interested in our uniformed groups of the Boys' and Girls' Brigades. We had a hall space available afternoons and one evening, so we painted and re-wired it to get it ready as another *Garden* setting, as an after school drop-in.

In trying to ensure this *Garden* was tailored to make the guests comfortable it has laptops with WiFi connections so they can update their Facebook pages; there are gaming opportunities on a Wii and PS3; table tennis, table football and an air hockey table. It includes places to sit and chat with maybe a hot chocolate or a cold drink. (We also took the opportunity to spread our links wider and have formed a partnership with our local Police team under the Redeeming Our Communities (ROC) initiative so that even more can be achieved from this single provision.)

But, a *Garden* on its own is not going to grow God's Kingdom. The plan is to build on this outreach event with a Sunday afternoon group who can get together for some fun and some biblical conversation, and also we're going to connect in with an existing Saturday evening monthly city wide Youth Worship event after an afternoon's fun together.

Example 4 The Retired

One setting we created was to provide a *Kitchen*, or small group for our older church members, but to also ensure it had some *Garden* opportunities to help them in reaching out to those they knew locally. We called it 'The Midweeker'. It was resourced by clergy as it helps the mix of folk in that group to have a variety of gatherings that might not have happened in another way. But we didn't want to just give a service on a Wednesday. It is not that there is anything wrong with it in itself, but it wouldn't encourage them to try engaging in a ministry or mission as a group.

Therefore we insisted on two things at the beginning. The first was that, across a month, at least two of the gatherings would be what we called a 'Thought For The Day' when anyone could lead the group around a Bible passage with their thoughts on it and minister to their friends. This was to encourage Bible reflection and 'meat eating' as mentioned in the earlier chapter, 'Mission isn't enough'.

The second insisted characteristic at the set up stage was to have them organise a social event they could invite a friend to about every 4 to 6 weeks.

To tie the whole thing together we produced a calendar card of the gatherings and social events they could give a friend. Their acquaintances in the main are in the previously churched part of the local population.

The social *Garden* events are simple things like a meal together at a restaurant or a trip to a local stately home and we even had a guided tour of the city's synagogue.

The variety of the gatherings in the church means 'The Midweeker' operates around the blurred edges of the *Dining Room* and *Kitchen*. It works with this group because so many who join in come from a 'churched' section of the local population, sometimes known by some as 'prodigal returners'. This is why one of the services we do in a month is fairly formal because it would still be familiar to the ones who come back. The other gatherings will then offer them a flavour of church they probably hadn't previously encountered. They seem to enjoy getting together, fellowship support is strong, outreach happens, they look at biblical application and they minister to each other as they worship in ways that suit them.

This was a designed setting that didn't exist before. It has shown the principle of thinking around a provision can achieve far more than just a good idea for a new service.

Across the first year the group doubled in size.

The flywheel focus of the
framework

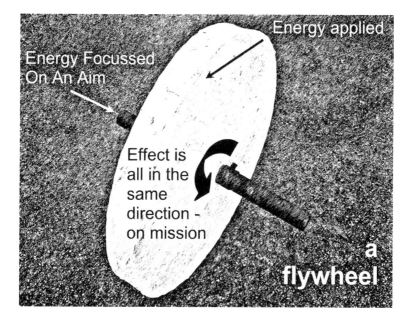

As we near the end I hope we can gain some confidence in maintaining energy effectively for the Kingdom by utilising the framework of *Gardens, Dining Rooms* and *Kitchens.*

Sometimes some of the ministries or gatherings we enable may be fun or good in themselves. But do they help in achieving our aims? A flywheel is a wonderful illustration of how effort could be put to the greatest effect, or how it can have a limited impact, or even make no contribution at all.

As churches grow, hopefully they will build up a momentum that will be self sustaining. But getting it moving will take effort.

A flywheel has the same characteristics.

To get it moving you need to apply regular effort. If you push in-line with the wheel all the energy you give will be absorbed by the wheel and it will begin to speed up. For the first period of time the amount of effort needed will be high and regular. But once it is revolving at speed it should only need occasional pushes to keep it moving.

However, if you instead try to get it moving by pushing at an angle against the side instead of in line with the rim, you will need to put in more energy for the same result. And if you were to stand to one side and push, but not on the flywheel at all, your effort will do nothing to help the flywheel keep moving and it will just start to slow down.

When our churches have limited resources it is crucial we start with an aim and then put our efforts in line with and into achieving that aim. Sometimes we just need to cease engaging with things that might stop us from doing what is important, because everything we do has an 'opportunity cost'.

If we do one thing, the time it takes up removes the opportunity to do something else. That is the 'opportunity cost' of some action. If we find we can't do something really important in our church that would work towards our aim, because resources are being used by something that doesn't promote our aim, we will need to reflect on what might be stopping us, and maybe stop doing that instead.

So, as with the flywheel, if we push in line then we get the greatest effect. If we come at it from an angle that's not really in line, we may waste some or most of that effort. And if we miss the aim and just push alongside somewhere then nothing will be achieved, or worse, doing the wrong thing may actually stop us from something that could be crucial.

We do the latter a lot in our churches.

As an example, having social events that have no reason other than just for fun are OK, but when you have a small number of people who are able and willing to organise and run them, planning in with *Dining Room* opportunities means you could achieve far more and the *Garden* events will now work towards your aim.

My hope is that, in times of limited resources, if we look at our churches using a framework like *Gardens, Dining Rooms and Kitchens,* we can build all we do on our aim.

A good place to begin is to analyse everything you already do. You can find some gaps in provision but more interestingly, you may discover that you are using resources on a project or ministry that achieves nothing.

And when you discover a ministry or programme that doesn't achieve anything towards your aim, it raises a really interesting situation: the possibility of cutting something out of your church's programmes.

When was the last time you stopped something the church was doing? It almost feels like a taboo question doesn't it?

If you are doing something that doesn't have positive results then it can be stopped. You might have to go through some pastoral processes so you don't hurt someone's feelings, but by streamlining, the church can become less busy and have more energy. Hopefully, we will find church leaders and church members who feel fulfilled and purposeful instead of being drained and desperately needing a holiday.

So the framework is a great place to start applying the principles behind *Gardens, Dining Rooms and Kitchens*. Patently it doesn't matter whether you use these names or maybe Guest, Friend and Family with Ministry and Mission or even just a, b and c, with a c1 and c2 for the process to work, but if you do change the labels to something that has more meaning in your context, use a series that form a simple journey so that it is easily memorised by your whole church. Remember a major point is that both your aim and your method need to be easily assimilated by everyone in your church.

The following exercise won't take too long, to get an initial idea on how you may be doing. You can even do it initially in the privacy of your study or lounge with some sheets of paper and some sticky notes if you are not yet sure if you want to introduce it to your church.

After you've gone through it quickly once to see what it might mean for your church, do it again with a small team and explain the principles behind it. Perhaps you could lend them this book first to keep everyone in the loop, and to help you all see the bigger picture: or get a church small group or team to utilise the separate study guide to come to some independent ideas?

So what should you do first as an exercise, to see what the implications of *Gardens, Dining Rooms* and *Kitchens* might be for your church?

Start by thinking of typical groups of people you connect with. It might be just as simple as the ones in the following picture: Elderly, Kids, Adults, Teens and Young Mum's, for example. Or you may be in a small village and only have contact with adults and the elderly. Start from there instead if that is your situation.

Over time you can then add those you may also want to reach in your local community. This will vary from location to location. In our instance there are two big communities we currently have no connection with, but that we might feel drawn towards later if we have some new members with special skills, or a new draw of the Holy Spirit. These would be a fairly new and large community from Poland and another that is Muslim, of varying nationalities. At the moment we don't have anyone with abilities and links with these two communities to begin something, nor do we have the resources. But if God thinks it is time and he wants us to do it, I'm fairly sure he will provide the people we will need.

So, the idea is to start with those groups of people you already connect with in some way. Write them on individual sheets and place them as your vertical axis for your grid. You can add those you don't currently have interaction with later.

Then write the various parts of the *Gardens, Dining Rooms and Kitchens* including the *Sink* and *Oven* onto another five sheets of paper and place those across the top. Fill in the rest of the grid with blank sheets.

Now treat yourself to a new stack of sticky notes and write everything you currently do: all your services, gatherings, courses, small groups etc on individual notes. An immediate challenge will be in thinking how they fit onto the grid, as that is where you now need to place them.

For instance, where will you put your main Sunday morning gathering? If it is not too complex and easy to follow, with teaching aimed at new or young Christians, and you have a congregation that is naturally welcoming, then might it be a *Garden* setting? If you think it should be, but isn't quite yet, then you may find you will want to modify it so it can be even more suitable for guests, if your leadership team agree with it being a *Garden* event. But remember, it needs to be suitable for a guest.

However, you may instead have a main Sunday service with lots of symbolism that brings a richness to your gatherings and which may need some explanation for a new person. You may begin to wonder if it is closer to a *Dining Room* or even a *Kitchen* setting. If so, do you have anything to enable people in earlier stages of faith to make use of and grow from the service?

And, wherever you place it, who is it for: adults, children, everyone? Do try to be honest with yourself about how it is now and you will begin to see gaps and overlaps.

As you progress through everything in which your church is currently involved and you begin to place them on the framework, you will discover some ministries or events that are really good, but that don't feed into anything. As an example, you may put on a phenomenal Carols and Readings service at Christmas that all your local people come to because they love to get into the 'Christmas spirit'. It may even be your biggest service of the year when you meet and give a message to hundreds more than usual. But do you have anything you can promote, maybe early in the New Year, that they can approach that will help them progress a little later on?

And you will also find some events with no obvious purpose. Either you can't place them on your grid or they are so different from anything else you're beginning to wonder why you do them. You don't need to remember the 'flywheel principle' to help explain why energy applied to these things does not help your aim, they will stand out on their own. Some other gatherings will be more nuanced and seem like they come at your aim from an angle. Maybe you won't stop them, but it could be a good reason to have a group look at possible modifications.

Our church members come up with some great ideas, but are they all useful or helpful? You may discover that using a framework which builds from Guest through Friend to Family, and that includes Ministry and Mission will enable you to answer some of these questions.

And a quick point on good ideas from church members.

I have a firm conviction that if a church is trying to do the right thing for God's Kingdom then he will bless it. Read the next chapter to see more fully what I mean. In blessing the church, God will provide the resources needed. That might be financial and you may need to ask for greater donations, but if it is his will it should be there. Equally, people with the right gifts are also required.

We can sometimes have enthusiastic folk offering good ideas for new ministries, you may even have some yourself. But they can't start until God provides what you need. If someone has a good idea and you can't yet start it because you don't have the funds or the people to do so, maybe it isn't yet the time. This principle will help you avoid feeling guilty that you can't start something yet even though it seems important. Of course you do have to assess the provision carefully. God might want you to do this new thing, but it might not seem possible because some people aren't yet being as generous with their time or finances as God wants them to be. In which case you may need to appeal to them, or yourself even, once more.

So, as you discover gaps, you can encourage folk to pick up the baton in some areas, to try and run with a new event that now fits into a strategy. If the resources aren't there yet, think about it again, ask God to provide what you need and look to see what else you might be able to do instead.

Maybe then we can work smarter, and not harder, for God and his Kingdom.

Chapter 16

Is it worth the effort?

I suspect there is a question that needs to be honestly faced when a church has got limited resources: 'Is it worth the effort?'

And if it is worth the effort, how can we encourage a church to see change and its challenges positively?

There is a wonderful story of three Kings going to war in the third chapter of 2 Kings. Israel, Judah and Edom go to war against Moab and after seven days the three armies run out of water. King Jehoshaphat of Judah is the only one who follows and acknowledges God in the whole group and he suggests they should enquire of God. One of the King of Israel's officers happens to know that Elisha is nearby and so they send for him.

Elisha arrives and probably wouldn't have spoken to them if Jehoshaphat hadn't been there. But after a short spell of time listening to the harp, Elisha hears God:

This is what the LORD says: Make this valley full of ditches. For this is what the LORD says: You will see neither wind nor rain, yet this valley will be filled with water, and you, your cattle and your other animals will drink. This is an easy thing in the eyes of the LORD; he will also hand Moab over to you. (2 Kings 3:16-18)

True to God's promise, the water arrived in a quantity no-one had dreamed of, more than needed. They asked for water and God sent them an abundance, as well as the victory over Moab they oddly hadn't asked for.

Providing water in a miraculous manner is easy for God. Giving more than is asked for is also what a loving parent does for a child. These are his children and he wants them to be blessed and thrive, so why wouldn't he want to demonstrate his grace?

But he did want the armies to do their bit first and dig a lot of ditches. It is quite a practical thing really. There is no point God sending water if there is nothing for it to flow into.

But, he still needs us to 'dig some ditches' to prepare for his blessing.

My own church faced some huge challenges with a building project approaching £1 million so I chose verse 3:16 as our verse for that year to help us see that efforts we would have to put in were 'just ditches' so God could bless us more.

This is what the LORD says: Make this valley full of ditches.

This episode in 2 Kings is such an encouraging event in the story of the relationship between God and his people that helps us when we face challenges. We know that God is love and filled with grace and longs to bless his children. As we have gone through this short book I hope we can see the need to engage with God and join as partners with him in mission, and to do our part in ensuring discipling opportunities are available if folk step over the threshold.

And this episode between God and the Kings illustrates so well the need for us to sometimes do something first which will enable God to do what he longs to be able to do. The principle of 'digging a ditch' can now give us a new outlook on resolving problems or engaging in hard work or challenges. No longer are we changing something or raising money or volunteering or having a meeting: we're just 'digging a ditch'.

This concept, if held and understood, can give a positive slant to everything a church may decide to engage with that might be hard, as we know it is now for the Kingdom and God's glory and so that his grace can follow.

God does want his church to thrive, but we all need to dig ditches for him to fill and do our part in this partnership he determined for the salvation of the world. My hope is that we all seriously engage in our own locality with the task before us. Analysing an aim, forming a strategy, and beginning to implement it, will mean God can then act in the way that is consistent with his character and motive of loving the whole world through his church. If this book helps you in that I couldn't ask for more. But I will just point out one last thing so you don't get diverted now you are so close to the end...

Chapter 17

And now what?

Maybe you have read this far and wondered, as you have pondered parts of it, whether or not you could apply some or all of the ideas into your own situation.

You may be beginning to agree with the principles of the last chapter and can now see that God does want to bless your church.

Are you now thinking about some more teaching or changes that won't be easy to bring about? Have you started to see which ditches may need digging so God could bring blessings?

However, soon you will probably be wondering if you did actually agree with some of the comments in this volume. Undoubtedly if I finished at the end of the last chapter you would have finished the book and put it down to ponder. And then the size of the task before you may begin to seem large. No-one else you know has read it yet and you are really busy, your church is exhausted and maybe you could just forget about it and keep doing things they way you have always done them. Then no-one will complain about changes either.

That's why I have included this last chapter, because without it you might not do anything.

You see, I have always been fascinated by something called 'cognitive dissonance'. It is that built in bit of our make-up that means we're uncomfortable when our actions don't match our beliefs. I almost suspect it is a psychologist's name for what we might call a conscience and it is particularly active on large decisions like the ones you may now be facing.

To help explain a little about what you may currently, or undoubtedly soon may be feeling, I'll use a different situation. Cognitive dissonance often affects us after expensive purchases.

Let's say you decide to buy a new car. It is a bit more than you budgeted for, actually it is quite a lot more than you budgeted for. But it is a great car. As you wake up the next day you wonder if you did the right thing. Should you have spent the extra on the package that included all the options, or gone for the base model you had seen at the original more affordable price? You feel a little uncomfortable.

And so begins your persuasion of yourself...

Doesn't the better MP3 radio you included mean when you take out the church young people, they can play their music from their phones and have a better time? Then there are the additional parking sensors: surely they will make it less likely you'll have a bump so your no-claims on the insurance should be safer and the policies get cheaper? And of all the extras, everyone knows it is easier to sell a second hand model that has them all, don't they?

Now you are feeling more comfortable.What did you feel and what did you then do?

That initial discomfort is called 'cognitive dissonance'. It was your actions not matching your beliefs. You felt uncomfortable because you spent more than you originally believed you wanted to afford. Then what did you do? You balanced your beliefs to your action by modifying your beliefs. You persuaded yourself your decision was based on some good facts and then you became comfortable in yourself.

And this is why I mention this now. Because as you have read this book you have probably felt that maybe you need to do something in your own church. But by now, or quite soon anyway, you may also start to think through some reasons not to. And then there will be the problem of persuading your own church to change how you deal with a newcomer, and the building isn't suitable, and... and.....

You will probably start to try and modify your original feelings, your original beliefs, because you don't fancy the actions that are necessary to balance them. This process won't necessarily be high on the conscious level, but could be floating near the subconscious. You may well begin to suffer from cognitive dissonance and feel uncomfortable about actions you are considering. And this will mean you could find you need to modify your beliefs instead of carrying out the actions. You will want to strive for balance, but what will you move to achieve it? Will you now try to do something about your church's provision or will you try to find as much fault as you can with this book?

I have no doubt some, maybe lots of this volume can be criticised, but does any of it make sense to you? What will you now do?

I mention this now because it is what I did when I realised I couldn't lead a church to give it a chance of growing God's Kingdom without bringing about some significant changes. It is what we always do when we're uncomfortable with how we feel on large decisions. Right now you are just about to decide whether or not you modify your belief, or change your actions to match what your new belief may be. I hope this last little chapter will help you recognise what your mind is just about to start doing, if it hasn't already.

Will you take some of the implications of this book and change the way your church acts towards growing its people as disciples of Christ in the context of mission, or will you ignore it, because you need to find a way to disagree with some of the ideas here?

I don't mind at all if you don't want to use this sort of method of strategising how your church engages with the un-churched or links mission more closely with your discipleship growth opportunities. But I do hope you can see a need to do something, because our God of self revelation is a missionary God who longs to see our personal transformation towards the character of his son, through the action of the Holy Spirit, as we become devoted disciples.

Feel totally free to liberate any of the ideas from this volume and change them into something that suits your context. You do have to find the right ways that suit your churchmanship and your people in your place at this time. I hope the reasoning behind the *Gardens, Dining Rooms and Kitchens* framework with the *Sink* and *Oven* can help you think through what you may need to create, amend or stop doing.

Maybe after everything, you will still quite reasonably decide not to use any of this but…

…let's remember something important …

The harvest is plentiful but the workers are few. Ask the Lord of the harvest, therefore, to send out workers into his harvest field.
Matthew 9:37-38

The importance of the simple idea of combining mission and discipleship is for it to be understood and put into practice by the many.

I asked the question about whether God would draw someone to a church if they weren't going to be helped become an active disciple. My very real hope is that the household imagery and simplified steps may assist your church to start to see things a little more strategically. But if you want to change it into steps 1, 2 and 3 with a 3a and 3b, I won't be offended.

You might have something like a great team of volunteers turning out, week in week out, to put on a group for toddlers and their carers, organising simple crafts and refreshments, offering a great resource for maybe a struggling or lonely single mum. What if they understood more could be achieved if they knew they were doing a great job in the *Garden*? Because once they know that, they will also know there are *Dining Rooms* and *Kitchens* that may suit one of their guests one day.

Once this, or a similar framework, becomes part of the DNA of your church then there is an opportunity to see many more 'labourers' being released, as people also become disciples.

And if you are a Church leader reading this and you want to try and bring some of the principles into practice, maybe to get a full set of opportunities initially for adults, don't try and do it yourself!

The whole point is to release people to make the whole body work better and for the individuals to discover every purpose God has prepared in advance for them. (Ephesians 2:10) You are probably already overworked, and as people change to become more like Jesus, they want to do the things he did. Disciples want to serve in ways relevant to their lives. Share this book with others or get them a copy for themselves. Perhaps have an initial team or your church small groups to utilise the study guide version.

If you find you need a course to help folk discover their ministry, try asking someone else to find one that suits, or maybe they could actually craft it and present it. There is every chance you already have someone who understands simple educational principles who could read a book and pull together a short course to suit the need.

I have a firm belief that God will provide the resources your church needs when you partner with him in his mission to his world. If you need a specific type of person, pray about it and ask him for them. God really is very generous. I remember my first church in paid ministry needed a keyboard player. We prayed and had a young couple join the church soon after. They were both keen and eager and she was a music graduate with skills across all sorts of instruments. The wonderful thing about God's grace and his desire to bless abundantly is that not only was she a keyboard player, but she formed a junior band and a youth orchestra and became the Youth Worker!

And why not! Is not our God a God of grace who is generous, who loves the world so much he was willing to give his Son for it?

If we choose to join in with the two commandments his Son thought were the most important and we resolve to take seriously his final commission to his Church, then wouldn't the Father want to bless our efforts?

I pray that as you now come to put down this book that you too will find time to pray about what you do next with God in his mission to his world.